THE CHAMPION WITHIN

Dr Samir Parikh is an eminent psychiatrist working in the field of mental health for close to three decades. He is Chairperson of the Fortis National Mental Health Program and Adayu Mindfulness, a Fortis Group Company. He is a prominent author, speaker and mentor.

Divya Jain is a sport psychologist and Head of Psychological Services for the Fortis National Mental Health Program. She works in the field of performance enhancement and mental health with elite and emerging athletes in individual and team sports, as well as with corporate organizations and schools.

*Dr Samir Parikh (Chief Mental Wellness Officer) and Divya Jain (Mental Wellness Officer) were appointed by the Indian Olympic Association to be part of the medical team that accompanied Team India for the 2024 Paris Olympic Games.

THE CHAMPION WITHIN

LIFE LESSONS FROM SPORT PSYCHOLOGY

SAMIR PARIKH
DIVYA JAIN

Published by
Rupa Publications India Pvt. Ltd 2025
7/16, Ansari Road, Daryaganj
New Delhi 110002

Sales centres:
Bengaluru Chennai
Hyderabad Jaipur Kathmandu
Kolkata Mumbai Prayagraj

Copyright © Samir Parikh & Divya Jain 2025

The views and opinions expressed in this book are the
authors' own and the facts are as reported by them; these
have been verified to the extent possible, and the publishers
are not in any way liable for the same.

All rights reserved.
No part of this publication may be reproduced, transmitted,
or stored in a retrieval system, in any form or by any means,
electronic, mechanical, photocopying, recording or otherwise,
without the prior permission of the publisher.

P-ISBN: 978-93-6156-081-1
E-ISBN: 978-93-6156-871-8

First impression 2025

10 9 8 7 6 5 4 3 2 1

The moral right of the authors has been asserted.

Printed in India

This book is sold subject to the condition that it shall not,
by way of trade or otherwise, be lent, resold, hired out, or otherwise
circulated, without the publisher's prior consent, in any form of
binding or cover other than that in which it is published.

Contents

Foreword *vii*

PART I

1. The Champion Mindset   3
2. Barriers to Peak Performance   12
3. The Anatomy of a Choke   18

PART 2

4. Dreams Are Free: Instilling Self-Belief   25
5. The Game Plan: Setting the Right Goals   34
6. Four Years for Nine Seconds: The Importance of Practice   43
7. A Step Ahead: Developing Anticipation   52
8. The Coach Within: Mastering Self-Talk   60
9. Quiet Eye: The Science of Focus   68
10. Seeing is Believing: Visualization for Performance   79
11. Fight, Flight or Freeze: Embracing the Adrenaline Rush   87

12.	Psyching Up! Psyching Down: Strategies for Self-Regulation	97
13.	Playing the Waiting Game: Getting into the Zone	106
14.	Taming Instinct: From Reacting to Responding	114
15.	To Di World: Lessons in Body Language	121
16.	Charms and Chances: Creating Your Own Luck	128
17.	Time Out: Breaks for Peak Performance	135
18.	The Balancing Act: Prioritizing Mental Recovery	146
19.	Rolling with the Punches: Overcoming Setbacks	156
20.	The Inner Drive: Revisiting Motivation	164
21.	Boos Don't Block Dunks: Handling Social Expectations	174
22.	The Sporting Spirit: Values for Success	184

PART 3

23.	A Big Day	195
24.	The Winning Attitude	201

Foreword

How many times have we been an audience to a sport, cheering for our favourite teams and favourite players, experiencing the highs and lows, the twists and turns as we witness the game unfold in front of our eyes?

Do you ever stop to think what might be going through the player's mind in those critical moments? Ever stop to think what *you* would do in that moment? And most importantly, what you could learn from these great athletes of our times?

There is no better metaphor for life than sport, and each of us has a champion within. You can be a student, an athlete, an entrepreneur or a professional—anyone with a dream to achieve.

Be a spectator to sport, yes. But in your own life, step onto the field and start playing. Play with your heart, win with your mind.

12. Psyching Up! Psyching Down: Strategies
    for Self-Regulation   97
13. Playing the Waiting Game: Getting into the Zone   106
14. Tuning Instinct: From Reacting to Responding   114
15. To Di World: Lessons in Body Language   121
16. Charms and Chances: Creating Your Own Luck   128
17. Time Out: Breaks for Peak Performance   135
18. The Balancing Act: Prioritizing Mental Recovery   146
19. Rolling with the Punches: Overcoming Setbacks   156
20. The Inner Drive: Revisiting Motivation   164
21. Boos in the Bleak Bunks: Handling Social
    Expectations   174
22. The Sporting Spirit: Values for Success   184

PART 3

23. A Big Day   195
24. The Winning Attitude   201

PART 1

What is the one quality
which you hold most important
for success?

1

The Champion Mindset

'Champions are brilliant at the basics.'

—John Wooden

30 June 2024. It's the morning after India won the Men's ICC T20 World Cup. The Indian team started out on the back foot, having lost three wickets in the first four overs. South Africa needed 30 runs off 30 balls. The match was all but lost. Yet, in sport—as in life—it's not over till it's over.

In stepped Jasprit Bhumbra, who had spent a large part of 2022–23 recovering from an injury, to send the South African team scrambling. Surya Kumar Yadav, who scored a meagre three runs with the bat, took a catch that will be spoken about for decades—and it probably turned the course of the game. Virat Kohli, who'd had a forgettable tournament up till that point, scoring his slowest ever T20 half-century, became the player of the match, anchoring the team towards victory. Finally, Rohit Sharma, still reeling from the defeat in the 2023 ODI World Cup final, captained the ship to victory.

The Game of Life

We all want to learn how to win. To be successful in life though, it's even more important to learn how to lose, to learn to get better, and to try again the next day. What better way to learn about success than through sport, where a player is confronted with winning and losing not just every day but every moment.

The Making of a Champion

For decades now, researchers have been trying to identify the secret sauce of success—what is it that makes or breaks a champion. In the field of sport, and in life, we can think of three kinds of preparation: mental, physical and technical. In a 1980s study involving Olympic athletes, it was found that mental readiness alone had a statistically significant link to the final Olympic ranking.

In this landmark research, it was found that a large percentage of Olympic athletes did not perform to their potential only because they were not prepared enough to deal with the distractions they faced.

There are two lessons to be gained from this study. The first is that when it comes down to the finish line, it's the mental skills that matter above all else. The second, and perhaps more important, is that we can *prepare* for the mental challenges that come our way. In most cases, these mental challenges aren't random. They're predictable, as are our responses to them. The question then becomes, just as you dedicate hours to hone your technique and skill to become physically stronger, how much time and effort are you really investing in the mental game?

Commitment

Lionel Messi once said, 'I start early and I stay late, day after day, year after year. It took me 17 years and 114 days to become an overnight success.'

It's no wonder, then, that across several researches the most consistent psychological 'success factor' that has been found is commitment. Why commitment? Because success doesn't come easy. Commitment to the sport or, for that matter, whatever we want to do in life is the driving force that motivates us to return to the training ground day after day. Success is not found in the quest for instant noodles. In a life filled with highs and lows, where others quit, champions persevere.

Competitiveness

That's right, champions don't just like to play, they like to win. However, this doesn't mean the desire to win at any cost. One who is competitive in the true spirit will never cross an ethical line to win.

Yes, it's important to compete with our own selves and get better every day, but here we're also talking about competitiveness with others. To be competitive means to have the desire to win and be able to put yourself out there. It means having the confidence to give it your all and enjoying the challenge of testing yourself against others. It involves having the courage to let other people see you try, and sometimes fail.

'Competitive' is not a bad word. It doesn't mean that you don't get along with your teammates or competitors.

The iconic photograph of Roger Federer and Rafael Nadal holding hands and crying says it all. It was at the Laver Cup in 2022, Federer's last match, which he chose to play *alongside* Nadal, and not against him.

Having someone to beat inspires us to dig deeper. Growth is stunted in the absence of healthy competition. Champions don't care if they're playing gully cricket or for the world cup, they play to win every single time.

Motivation

Motivation is the fuel for success—it's what people use to begin and sustain any pursuit. All of our actions, even the seemingly irrelevant ones, are bound by motivation. Motivation answers the 'why': Why do you do what you do? Champions have the answer; and while this can be different for different people, the answer has to come from within.

When people are motivated by external rewards—money, recognition or acceptance, it's likely one might feel choice-less or stressed. While external rewards are important, champions are motivated by something beyond them. It's the internal rewards that champions crave: a challenge to overcome, the satisfaction of learning and getting better, or the joy of the activity itself! While external rewards are few and far between, the internal rewards are ours for the taking, every single day. Seek internal rewards, and every moment will be an opportunity to keep that fuel tank topped up. And the best part? Going for those internal rewards is also the best way to reach your external gains. It's a win-win!

A Vision for Success

Reading this title, you might imagine standing on a podium, or buying a big car or a house. But we're not talking about a vision *of* success; we're talking about a vision *for* success. What do you need *to do* to reach that podium? To excel, no matter the field, it's always the process, always the journey that matters. After all, while driving, your focus can't be on the destination, it has to be on the road ahead of you and the next turn you have to take.

Champions have a vision of what it takes to succeed, and vision here is not just a vague idea or thought, but the ability to *see* the process. Visualize what it takes to reach your peak—whether it's a single performance or a larger quest. Interestingly, control of performance imagery has been directly related to a high performance level at the Olympic Games.

Quality Practice

This is a no-brainer. The quest for excellence requires one to hone their skills, and this means quality practice. Champions engage in deliberate practice. It's not just about stacking up the hours; every practice session has well-established goals. It involves improving strengths and also working on weaknesses. It involves training the body *and* the mind. Champions don't just practise skill execution in an ideal setting—they practise their performance with all its pressures, surprises and imperfections.

Coping with Pressure

What do penalty shootouts and super overs have in common? Even though they're often used to determine who wins, they don't really test the technical prowess of the players beyond a point. What they're really testing is a team's ability to keep its cool under pressure.

Any big performance comes with its pressures and expectations—if it's important, the pressure is unavoidable. Champions feel this pressure too. The difference is that they use this pressure to perform even better. Where many choke, champions clutch the moment. The difference isn't necessarily in the number of points a champion wins—the real difference lies in *which* points they win. They're usually the ones that matter more, the ones that come with more pressure.

A Realistic Evaluation

We all have a little scientist residing in our minds, feeding us explanations for why something happens: 'Did I make a mistake, or was it bad luck?' This is not always an objective assessment, and it depends on perspective. Some of us tend to blame poor outcomes on bad luck and good outcomes on effort; others do the exact opposite.

Champions don't lie to themselves; they don't make excuses for their performance. They own up to their mistakes and take the credit for their successes. Their attributions are therefore what psychologists call 'internal' and 'stable'. It's what gives champions a sense of control over their performance.

A realistic evaluation means being able to look yourself in the mirror and accepting your strengths and weaknesses as they are. After all, if you don't know where you stand, how do you know where to go next?

Confidence

'My life is my message—nothing is impossible.' These words by M.C. Mary Kom say it all. Ask champions what the most important mental quality for success is, and the unequivocal answer you're going to get is confidence. It's the confidence that helps you stay relaxed under pressure, focus better, set high targets, put in more effort, and persevere.

Game Awareness

'Even though there's no physical contact in tennis, there is a lot of eye contact.' These words by Novak Djokovic are from when he spoke about how he was always aware of his opponents' expressions—recognizing flickering moments of weakness which he could exploit to his advantage.

In the world of sport, it's called game awareness. But the same applies to situational awareness in every other aspect of life as well. Even as you focus on your process, your technique, you still need to keep an eye out for changes in the external environment. Truly understanding your field, recognizing patterns, being aware of changing trends, reading your opponents, developing the ability to think outside the box, and factoring in external variables are all essential if you want to stay one step ahead of the crowd.

Social Skills

This one may come as a bit of a surprise, but when it comes to success, social skills matter—even if it's an individualistic sport that you're playing. Even an individual athlete has an entire entourage that supports them behind the scenes. Given the fact that we're faced with social interactions on an everyday basis, having the right skills to navigate these situations can help find reciprocity, avenues for collaboration, manage conflicts and build social support systems. The ability to manage social situations well can also be a huge boost to our confidence.

The Next Steps

Champions are not born, they're made. We all have a champion within us. To perform at our peak requires our mind and body to work together in sync with our thoughts, emotions, values and actions, which should all be aligned towards the same objective.

Now that we've identified the psychological makings of a champion, in the next chapter we're going to recognize the common pitfalls we experience on our path to success. We'll talk about the common patterns of thinking, feeling and relating that get in our way, and decode the manner in which they impact our performance. The rest of the book will then deep-dive into simple, specific skills and strategies—the basic building blocks of success—that you can adopt to unleash the champion within.

Does your own mind ever
get in the way of you
performing at your best?

2
Barriers to Peak Performance

Nothing of what we've shared in Chapter 1 should come as a surprise. We all know how important it is to practise, to be motivated, and to be confident. So then, why do we so often miss the mark? What stops us from achieving those heights of success we aspire to?

The problem is not one of intent. What we have to realize is that our mind is like a tool, and just like with any tool, we need to learn the right techniques to use it well. Most often, we take our mind for granted, picking up strategies for thinking and responding through hearsay. Inadvertently, this lack of training sometimes results in subtle errors that have far-reaching ramifications in our quest for success.

I Must Be Perfect

Perfectionism really can be a double-edged sword. On the one hand, it keeps us on our toes; it pushes us towards working harder and doing better every day. It drives us to work tirelessly in our quest to hone our craft. To attain a level of mastery is perhaps one of our greatest yearnings.

On the flip side, though, this very need for perfectionism can turn against us. Let's face it, it's not possible to achieve standards of perfectionism each and every time. Mistakes are inevitable, and there's always room for growth. When being 'perfect' becomes the target, every mistake we make serves as a blow to our confidence. The fear of failure creeps in gradually, and our mind comes up with a simple solution—'if I don't try, I can't fail.' The opposite of this, trying too hard can also have its fair share of negative consequences, something we'll go further into in the next chapter.

What Will People Say?

Human beings have a need to belong. That need sometimes translates into a need for social acceptance, as a pathway to belonging. 'Validation' is a word that is increasingly being heard in pop psychology narratives rampant on social media.

When we fear the judgements of others, we fear the emotion of shame. It shows up in subtle ways, such as when we hear ourselves say, 'I don't want to disappoint my loved ones.' Shame is a very powerful emotion, one that we will do just about anything to avoid. And so, when we get preoccupied with what other people are going to say about us, the task no longer matters as much. Instead, our focus shifts from performing the task at hand to managing our own impression. Sometimes this can lead us to once again making excuses or avoiding the situation altogether. Or, it can make us try too hard, overwhelm us and interfere with our ability to perform.

This Right Here Is a Do or Die

We tend to think of success as a cross-sectional event—a single moment that will change our lives forever. For some it's a medal at the Olympic Games, for others, it could be bagging a major gig, cracking an entrance exam or getting a dream job. And so, we direct all our efforts towards realizing this moment.

The problem is, success is longitudinal, the outcome of several wins and losses. And when we think of any moment as a make or break in our lives, not only is it unrealistic, it also creates tremendous pressure. In trying to clinch that moment, rest and recovery take a backseat. Tensions rise, as do the mistakes. Expectations soar, we lose perspective, and failure looms as a threat.

It's Not Fair!

There are plenty of situations in our lives that are not in our control. These only become exaggerated when we perform in environments that are different from the ones we are familiar with. While we do train our skill, we don't pay much heed to the environment in which we train, or other situational factors that may come in the way. Some of them may seem unfair as well. And so, when the uncontrollables kick in, which they are bound to, we have a hard time adjusting. This can lead to thoughts of blame or feelings of helplessness, both of which are counterproductive to peak performance.

I Have to Win

Most of our efforts are usually in pursuit of a target, something we want to achieve. It is, after all, these goals that motivate us to work hard, day in and day out. They serve as the vision board that guides our everyday choices and actions.

Unfortunately, no matter how hard we strive, results aren't always in our control. For us to come first depends not just on our efforts, but also on someone else coming second. Thus, when a particular result is what we're after, the goalpost keeps shifting.

Another problem with result orientation is that it takes us away from the present moment. Thinking about the result takes us into the future. Without us even realizing, it becomes a distraction that interferes with the way we perform. When the scoreboard becomes all-consuming, we take our eye off the ball.

I Feel Overwhelmed

During a big event, we also experience big emotions. Because of the heightened state we're in, every emotion feels stronger. The problem is that these emotions often make us impulsive. The term 'rage quitting' has gained increasing prominence in our vocabulary over the last couple of decades. And it's not just anger, other emotions can also overwhelm us. In fact, the anticipation of winning can lead to so much excitement that it can make us respond prematurely, and lead to making more unforced errors. Each of these emotions—joy, anger, fear, sadness, guilt, shame or surprise—can change our internal environment and our focus. They can boost our energy or sap us of it.

What If?

When facing challenges, our mind likes to prepare. It likes to come up with every scenario that can go wrong. Now this can be very helpful in preparing us for contingencies. What about the things we can't control though? That's where our mind goes into overdrive. We aren't able to accept and let go of the things we can't control. Instead, our mind likes to think about them over and over again. Worry becomes the (unhelpful) way of giving us a perception of control, making us feel like we're doing something about it. Inevitably, these thoughts make us feel more and more nervous, and take away our focus from the things that are actually in our control. Consequently, the confidence too takes a nosedive.

What's the Point?

Life is not a vending machine that you put in a coin, press a button and get what you want. Yes, actions have consequences, and yes, efforts yield results; but life is not so linear. There will be times when even the best efforts will result in failure. There will also be times when things come easy, only to be taken away. And there will be times when things seem too difficult. So, while success can take time, the one thing life does give out freely are chances. Giving up hope is probably the single greatest barrier to success. Life rewards tenacity. In the famous words of George Moore, 'A winner is just a loser who tried one more time.'

Can you recall an instance when you choked under pressure?

3

The Anatomy of a Choke

Wimbledon 1993. Jana Novotná had beaten second seed Martina Navratilova to set up a championship clash against Steffi Graf. After having taken a set each, Novotná was leading the third set 4–1 and was serving at game point. If she won that point, she would be up 5–1, a lead almost impossible to overturn. Instead, she double-faulted. This unforced error tipped the scales and Steffi Graf won the next five games on the trot, eventually winning the championship. This is considered to be one of the greatest chokes in sporting history.

It isn't unusual for people to choke under pressure. Blanking out during an exam even after having prepared really well is a common example. Making unforced errors in a sport, forgetting lines on stage, fumbling during a meeting—these are all versions of a choke, derailing us right when it matters the most.

To learn to overcome the choke, it's helpful to understand it a bit better. Stress doesn't directly result in us performing poorly. Instead, it leads to a domino effect, which involves our body physiology, our thoughts and emotions, and finally, our behaviour. Each of these topples in such quick succession that they seem like they're all happening at once. Understanding the anatomy of the choke can help us deconstruct and eventually break out of this pattern.

First: The Perception of Threat

Remember, not everyone responds to a situation the same way. Some people may feel extremely anxious on a stage, while others may feel entirely at home. Those who experience a sense of threat feel more stressed. But how does a person determine this threat? They evaluate the situation based on how well they believe they can deal with it, or the extent to which they feel they have the resources to cope. If the situation challenges their capacity, the body proceeds to step two—the fight or flight response.

Second: Fight or Flight

The fight or flight response refers to the physiological impact of stress. When confronted with a stressful situation, the body's hypothalamic-pituitary-adrenal axis is activated. The result is an increase in cortisol levels and the activation of the autonomic nervous system's stress response.

This is when the heart rate and blood pressure start increasing. Higher levels of glucose are secreted to allow for quicker energy. Our breathing becomes shallow and rapid to increase oxygen intake. Our pupils dilate to let in more light, so we can see better. Our sweat glands get more activated. Digestion slows down, and we may experience 'butterflies in the stomach'. Our muscles tighten up, preparing for action. The amygdala, the emotional centre in the brain, also fires up. We feel more alert, more vigilant, and our emotions become heightened.

Third: Changes in Thinking

We're not used to feeling all these things in our everyday practice and training. So when we do feel this heightened stress, our mind perceives it as something negative—perhaps a sign that we are scared or unprepared in some way.

Our focus narrows to the single point of threat in our environment, limiting our cognitive flexibility. We feel stuck if we're not immediately able to come up with a solution. Our ability to think laterally is impacted.

In fact, this state of high arousal also temporarily impairs the functioning of our pre-frontal cortex, which is responsible for a lot of our thinking and decision making.

High-stress situations can interfere with our memory as well, which is why sometimes we feel like we've gone blank. Being in this kind of head space, past memories of similar stresses come flooding back to us, and the negative emotions of fear, anger, guilt and shame stack up.

Fourth: Behavioural Changes

The stress response culminates in poor performance only if it impacts our behaviour—which is exactly what happens when we choke.

An example of this is when stress increases our muscle tension, causing the grip on an object we're holding to tighten, no longer allowing for the flexibility or range of motion we typically require to complete a task. Another way it manifests is that as the body is more energized, the pitch, pace and volume of our speech increases. Movements too become faster. As a response to this, sometimes we double down, forcing ourselves to play slower than usual. All of these can disrupt our rhythm, disconnecting our mind from our body.

As we start to feel more self-conscious, we are no longer able to focus on the task at hand. Instead, our focus shifts inwards, on managing our own emotions. We start doubting ourselves, second-guessing our every move. From acting in a way that sets us up for success, our efforts shift toward avoiding failure. We behave in a way that's more 'safe' and, in the process, do things differently from our usual methods. So, for instance, rather than aiming for the sidelines—which is what you would normally do when playing confidently—you now hesitate. In your decision to play safe, you end up hitting the shot bang in the centre, making it easy for the opponent to return the shot with a smash of their own. The decision to 'play safe' rather than playing free ends up costing you point.

In moments of psychological discomfort, our tendency is to respond in one of two ways. Either we try too hard or we try too little. Trying too hard is what we've spoken about previously. How does our mind try too little? It checks out. It disconnects from the present moment because it's unable to tolerate the discomfort it experiences. We just want to be done with it and run away from the situation. We might, once more, start behaving more impulsively. We may not give enough time to planning, strategizing and executing, and instead, we might start making jokes or making excuses.

The game is no longer important. We're willing to do just about anything to not feel bad in that moment.

In that moment, you may try too hard and fail. Or, in avoiding the negatives, you end up making choices that don't always align with your long-term goals and values. Each of these impacts your self-confidence, which makes you more susceptible to threats.

Breaking Patterns

Ok, so that was the bad news. Now for the good news: we can change how we respond to difficult situations. The chain reaction we've spoken about just now isn't inevitable. In fact, it's possible to break it every step of the way, which is what the rest of the book is going to help you do.

You can change the way you perceive situations, so that you don't experience them as threatening in the first place. You can train your mind and body to reverse the fight–flight response. You can bring your focus within your control, rather than letting it be guided by fear and anxiety. You can change your behaviours by substituting avoidance with acceptance.

We started this chapter by talking about Jana Novotná's choke in 1993. But that's not the full story. Novotná came back, year after year. She lost the final once more against Martina Hingis in 1997, before finally winning the Wimbledon title in 1998. Novotná's legacy is not that of a choker. The world remembers her as a winner, through and through.

PART 2

> Has the fear of failure ever stopped you from trying something you've always wanted to?

4

Dreams Are Free: Instilling Self-Belief

'If my mind can conceive it, if my heart can believe it—then I can achieve it.'

—Muhammad Ali

Muhammad Ali, the self-proclaimed 'greatest', is perhaps one of the best lessons in self-belief. Not only was he the undisputed champion of heavyweight boxing, he also had the courage to stand up for what he believed was right, outside the ring.

Why Self-Belief Matters

We've all heard the trope 'believe in yourself', but when it comes to how we perform, does it really matter? The answer is yes. Unequivocally, yes. In fact, a person's belief in their abilities is one of the greatest predictors of success.

When we believe in ourselves, we dare to dream. We set

higher, more challenging goals for ourselves, and then work harder towards achieving them. If I believe in my ability to reach the ball, I'm going to make that dive to catch it. I'm not going to sit around calculating the odds of success, I'm simply going to give it my all and go for it. And, who knows, two times out of ten I may catch it as well! Without that self-belief, I become a mere spectator to my own life, watching the ball go by, thinking, 'what's the point, I wasn't going to catch it anyway.' Without that self-belief, we make our dreams smaller and our worlds narrower. Without that self-belief, we give up sooner.

Look in the Mirror

There are two parts to the term self-belief: self and belief. The belief can't come without first knowing the self, and we need to know what we're to believe in.

We see the world through the lens of our own self, whether we realize it or not. How we feel about ourselves has a direct impact on how we see the world around us. So if we don't take the time to get to know ourselves, we're going to feel lost. We'll make the same mistakes over and over, without realizing the role we might be playing in them. We'll miss out on opportunities for self-correction, to make positive changes and take control of our lives.

Who am I? Why am I doing what I do? What are my priorities? What are my values? What are my strengths? Where do I tend to falter? How prepared am I? What strategies do I use to cope with challenges? What am I thinking or feeling at the moment? How relaxed or tense is my body? What am I conveying through my body language?

The self as a concept includes all of the ideas, perceptions and values that define 'me'. So, to build self-awareness, take a moment to get to know yourself better. Pause and shift your gaze within. Become an observer and start noticing what's going on within you.

Test Yourself

When we're talking about self-awareness, the idea is not to become an armchair thinker, building castles in the air. Our sense of self comes from our experiences and the ways in which we see ourselves interact with the world around us.

We don't need a report card to tell us how we've performed. If we're self-aware, we already know what our grades will be, on the day we go in for the exam. If there's a big mismatch between our expectations and reality, then we've actually got a bigger problem on our hands. When our perception of who we are doesn't match our experiences, it creates distress and anxiety.

To bridge the gap between the real and the ideal self, we need to get to know the real first. And here, to be honest with ourselves is the most important thing. Whether we're winning or losing, whether we've prepared well enough or not, we can't lie to ourselves. It simply won't work. The key is self-evaluation. Know where you stand so you can dig your heels in. Whether it's mock examinations, speaking in front of the mirror before big presentations, or practice matches, keep testing yourself. It's the only way you'll feel prepared for the tests that life throws your way.

Be Open to Feedback

No matter how much we reflect and introspect, we still have some blind spots—things that others see in us that we don't recognize ourselves, or perhaps patterns that we fall into time and again, without realizing why. This is where the power of feedback comes in.

You might have heard of Newton's third law: Every action has an equal and opposite reaction. Everything we do has consequences, and life gives us constant feedback. We only have to keep our eyes and ears open to receive it; the feedback will come.

Now, there are certain conditions and caveats to keep in mind when taking feedback.

The first is to take a balanced approach to both accolades and criticisms. Getting swept up with either or neglecting one or the other, both are going to give us a skewed perspective. Give equal weightage to the positives and the negatives.

The second is to reflect on the source of the feedback. The idea is not to give in to the criticisms of every troll or commentator, or to even get carried away by every 'like' on our posts. Don't pay heed to anonymous critique, but take it with a pinch of salt. Don't indulge in speculations; take feedback from the results of your performance, the responses of your peers, opinions from experts, and well-meaning conversations with a guide or mentor.

The third is to not react to every piece of criticism that comes your way. Highs and lows are a part of life; we're bound to have good days and bad days. Knee-jerk reactions to every comment that comes our way isn't the way to go. Instead, introspect on the feedback you get. Notice if there are patterns, if the same feedback is coming to you from various avenues. Match it to the knowledge you have about your own self. If you find value in it, learn from it. If not, let it go and move on from it.

Not Just Criticisms, Compliments Too!

Just like you have to be open to criticism, keep yourself open to compliments as well. Sounds quite easy and straightforward, but you'll be surprised by how many people struggle to take a compliment. When someone says something nice about us, we often get awkward, shy away, or trivialize our efforts. Accepting criticism and compliments are two sides of the same coin, and we need to be able to do both. So next time someone gives you a compliment, don't look away. Instead, soak it in. Make eye contact, smile, and say thank you. After all, you deserve the win.

As a side note, make it a habit to compliment other people around you as well. You'll be surprised at how much this simple act can contribute to your own confidence.

Celebrate Your Uniqueness

A Sachin Tendulkar comes around only once. One Sachin can win games for the team, undoubtedly, but we'd be mistaken to believe that a team of 11 Sachin Tendulkars could win us a match. Quite the contrary! We need batters with different skill sets and temperaments, bowlers, wicketkeepers as well. In trying to compare ourselves to somebody, there's a risk that we may never nurture our own individuality.

We might believe that comparing ourselves to other

people can motivate us to work harder. And yes, idolizing a role model can inspire us to do better. But there's a difference between learning from others and comparing ourselves to others. *Nothing kills confidence like comparison does.*

While this tendency to compare has always been around, it's become so much more pronounced with the rise of social media. We find ourselves constantly comparing ourselves with the curated lives of other people—we equate skill and success with views and likes. The number of followers we have has become the measure of our self-worth! And in this race for popularity, we often find ourselves trying to clone other people, letting go of our own selves.

To build your self-confidence, don't let comparisons, either online or offline, define you. Set your own yardstick. The aim today is just to be better than you were yesterday. Don't let others choose your goals or define your self-worth. Find what it is that *you* are good at, and be proud of it. Give your real self a chance.

Rely on Your Strengths

From an evolutionary perspective, our minds are trained to focus on what is wrong—it helped our ancestors remember where the threats lay and how to survive in an environment fraught with danger. While the environment around us is no longer the same, our minds are still wired similarly.

We often spend time working on the things we're weak at, while taking our strengths for granted. In critical moments of a competition, or when things get difficult, our tendency is to do something different, something we don't normally do and that doesn't come naturally to us. Someone whose strength it is to attack suddenly turns defensive, trying to play it safe. Somebody who rallies to build a point starts smashing every shot they can. This is often why we choke under pressure—we stop trusting our strengths.

We don't need to be good at everything to be successful. If you really think about it, we need just one or two skills that we're good at to be successful. Would a batter spend most of their time in the nets practising bowling? Probably not. Because it just doesn't matter. What matters is the one strength that you do have. It's this strength that needs to be sharpened even further, because it's this strength that holds the key to your success.

The right body language, visualizations and self-talk can also play a significant role in enhancing our self-confidence. Given their importance and import in several aspects of performance, we've dedicated entire chapters to these skills.

'What if I Become Overconfident?'

Before we end this chapter on self-belief, it's important to address this concern, because it's one we come across rather often. 'What if confidence turns into overconfidence?', or 'Never believe that you have achieved, because then you'll become complacent.'

Well, the truth is that overconfidence and underconfidence are two sides of the same coin. They are both rooted in a lack of self-awareness and self-belief. What we call overconfidence is simply a defence, a way of lying to our own selves and others. A person who is overconfident is in fact not confident at all.

Confidence, on the other hand, is rooted in effort

and awareness. All the strategies discussed above will be meaningless if there's no training to back them up. So, go ahead and back yourself. If you've worked hard and prepared well, then the sky's the limit!

> **Podium Finish**
>
> 1. Allow yourself to dream, and back your ability to achieve those dreams.
> 2. There is no self-belief without self-awareness. Be honest and truthful to your own self.
> 3. Don't try to be like everybody else. Embrace your uniqueness and strengths.

Ever felt you could have approached a goal differently?

5
The Game Plan: Setting the Right Goals

'I think goals should never be easy, they should force you to work, even if they are uncomfortable at the time.'

–Michael Phelps

Swimmer Michael Phelps, who has won a record 28 Olympic medals, learnt his first lessons in goal setting at the age of 11. That's when he says his Olympic dream began. At the age of 11, he told his coach he wanted to win an Olympic medal, and his coach responded, 'Ok, in four years you can do that.' He then asked the young Phelps to write his goals down on a sheet of paper. The rest is the stuff of legend.

Setting a goal for ourselves is the most obvious first step in our journey to success. It's also often the most neglected first step. Yes, we all have dreams—it could be to win an Olympic medal or to become a chief experience officer (CXO), amongst others. But the path to achieving any dream is via the goals that we set for ourselves. There is a science to setting these goals, and the right goals are hugely influential when it comes to building confidence, focus and resilience.

Own Your Goals

The first thing to keep in mind is that the goals you set for yourself should be your own. Yes, we all have expectations to live up to—our family, friends, teachers, and peers, they all want what they believe is best for us. Unfortunately, there's no end to expectations, and there's no end to comparisons.

In fact, researchers have outlined two types of orientations when it comes to success. The first is task orientation, where our goal of action is to develop a sense of mastery, learning or improvement. When we are ego-oriented, on the other hand, we feel successful when we outperform others, especially when we put in less effort than them! When goals are easily achievable, and the self-belief high, there's no problem. But in the face of adversity, those with task orientation are going to keep trying, keep striving, while those with ego orientation may choose to avoid such challenging situations altogether. As an added benefit, a higher task orientation also means that you're probably going to enjoy what you are doing more.

So, resist the temptation to set goals that you believe others expect you to. Don't focus on merely outperforming others. Instead, let your goals be your own. When your loved ones see you working hard to fulfil your own aspirations and being content with your own choices, the appreciation will follow.

Break 'em Down

Larger goals can sometimes feel daunting, and our tendency then becomes to escape doing the work at all. Here is when you have to break down your goals. While long-term goals are what inspire you to work hard, it's the short-term and immediate goals that give you the direction you need. Think of a long-term goal as winning a football match. The short-term goal then would be getting the ball into the actual goalpost in those 90 minutes. The posts with the white net is how you know where to aim the ball, which is where to direct your efforts.

Short-term goals allow us to be agile and adapt well to changing circumstances, while long-term goals can take years to achieve. So, the short-term goals can be those that you set yourself for a single practice session, a single day, a week, or a month. Phelps broke down his long-term goals into much smaller steps. For instance, when his goal was to reduce his 200 metre butterfly time by two seconds in a year, he would set monthly goals to shave off fractions of a second. Talk about short term!

Short-term goals are the steps of the ladder to success. When things get difficult, all you have to do is put one foot in front of the other.

The Right Kind of Challenge

You must've heard people say 'aim for the stars; even if you miss, you'll reach the moon.' This can encourage us to set very high, ambitious goals for ourselves. And yes, in general, it's good to set a high target for oneself—if we don't, we're already preparing for failure.

There is a caveat here though. We must also remember that we're more likely to do things that we are good at. We're more likely to *enjoy* things that we're good at, and that increases our commitment to the task. And here's where finding the right balance comes in. Setting very high targets that we're more likely to fail to reach may lead us to becoming disheartened. Even if we do very well, but it's not at the level we want it to be, our mind perceives it as a failure, as though we're not good enough.

So, when setting goals, give yourself an opportunity to win. It doesn't have to be a walkover or an easy win. But it does have to be something that you can achieve if you put in the right effort. Aim for a target that you can likely achieve about seven out of 10 times, if you put your mind to it. This is going to make you *want* to keep trying and getting better with every passing day. We need our goals to be challenging, yes, but achievable as well.

Think Process, Not Result

It's easy to think of goals in terms of what we can achieve—a medal, a rank, a score. These are result-oriented goals, where we're looking to achieve a certain kind of outcome. The problem here is that the results aren't always in our control. Your coming first doesn't just depend on your own scores, it also depends on someone else coming in second. We may not realize it, but focusing on the result can also become a significant source of distraction during our performance. After all, results are always in the future, never in the present moment, while we're performing. Thinking about them takes us away from what it is that we're actually supposed to do to achieve those results.

So rewire your goals to focus on the process, on the pathway to achieving those goals. For instance, for Michael Phelps, meticulously practising his starts and turns was important, since these significantly impacted his timings. The trick is not just to set your mind to winning, but rather to set your mind to playing the winning game.

Do Your 'Best'?

If we aren't setting goals about winning, what we often end up doing is telling ourselves to 'do my best'. While this does sound like a positive and supportive goal, it can actually end up doing more harm than good!

The problem with a 'do your best' kind of goal is that it lacks specificity. My definition of best is different from yours. For one person, doing well may mean an 80 per cent score, while for another, it may mean a 95 per cent. In fact, I may not be clear on my own idea of what it means to do my best. It just becomes one more sentence of random chatter that's going on in my mind. One that may or may not add pressure, but certainly doesn't provide any direction.

Instead, take a moment to think about what it means to do your 'best'. What kind of footwork would it involve, or what kind of strategy? What kind of attitude or attentional focus would it require, and what are the specific behavioural patterns you need to follow to achieve it? Might sound a bit too complicated at first, but if you can't do it right now, there's no way your mind will know what the best is when you're actually in that situation.

Hence, make sure that your goals are specific. Specific

goals will ensure that you and your entire support system work towards the same goal. It will keep you clear and objective and help break down your task into meaningful, achievable units. Most of all, remember that goals are not just a source of motivation. More than anything else, they're a beacon giving us a sense of direction.

The Journey or the Destination?

Simply put, our goal is the destination, but no conversation about reaching our destination is complete without taking a moment to talk about the journey. And what is this journey? It's the values that we choose to live our lives by. Each of us may choose to live by a different set of values, but it's crucial to know which of them truly matter to us. Is it honesty? Hard work? Kindness? Loyalty? There could be so many more.

In your quest to achieve your targets, make sure that you are cognizant of the values you hold important. When things get difficult, or perhaps when conflicts arise, it's these values that will inspire you and make your choices clear. We'll be talking about values a lot more in depth in the later chapters, because when it comes to success, they do really matter. But in the meanwhile, as you set your goals, make sure that they are goals that make you proud—goals that are aligned to your true, authentic self.

Watch Them Come True

Don't just think about your goals, put them out into the world as well. Take a leaf out of Phelps' book and write your goals down, and then visualize them as they come true.

What's important to keep in mind while visualizing your goals is not just to think about winning; instead, incorporate all the strategies that we've spoken about so far. Break them down to every precise detail, focus on the process of your winning performance, feel the energy, the commitment, and the focus as you perform. Visualize not just competitions, but your training sessions as well, right down to every single move. Visualize the hurdles you may experience, and more importantly, how you will overcome them. Visualize every moment of the journey from the start to the finish, so when the time comes, you're better prepared to make it all come true.

The Power of Purpose

Motivation is the driving force behind all our behaviours, so choose your motivation wisely. Not everybody is motivated by the same things. For your goals to be powerful, you need them to be personally meaningful to you. Think big, think long-term. In this pursuit, connecting these goals to something larger than your own self can also help, such as how you can contribute to your family, your community, or a cause you believe in.

It's not about adding pressure or expectations, but rather about drawing strength from something bigger than yourself. When you are harnessing the power of purpose, your motivation won't wax and wane with a single positive or negative outcome. It's going to keep you steady on your path, give you the ability to persevere despite the odds, and enable you to stay committed to this larger vision.

Podium Finish

1. Goals aren't about the destination alone. They shape our entire journey.
2. Own your goals. Make them specific, achievable and challenging.
3. Focus on the processes, not just the results.

Do you practise regularly?

6

Four Years for Nine Seconds: The Importance of Practice

'Practice doesn't make perfect. Only perfect practice makes perfect.'

—Vince Lombardi

Going into a meeting or an interview, how often do we really practise what we're going to say? We often tend to rely on our experience. Some of us may prefer mental rehearsals rather than really putting ourselves out there. For some it seems unnecessary, for others, intimidating.

What separates athletes and performing artists from most other professionals is their emphasis on practice: spending hours every day in the nets, even after becoming the best in the world. There's a lot to learn from this work ethic of elite athletes, and we do believe that all of us, regardless of our profession or stage of life, can learn and do better if we're open to learning.

The Audience Effect

There's a concept in social psychology known as the 'audience effect'. What it means is having others observe us, even passively, has a significant impact on our performance. Take a moment to think about how the presence of an audience would impact your own performance. Do you perform better or worse?

The answer usually isn't linear. Interestingly, when in front of an audience, people tend to perform a simple task better, and a complicated task worse. Put another way, we're likely to do better at a task we're good at and worse at a task we're not good at.

This is where the importance of repetition comes into play. When we're under pressure, we're likely to do what we're most likely to do, that is, what we usually do most often. During moments of heightened arousal, which could take the form of fear or excitement, our most dominant, automatic response takes over. Which is why, if you're learning a new skill or technique, you may not actually be able to implement it during a performance, reverting instead to what you have been doing earlier. It may be a flawed technique, one that you're trying to get rid of, but if it's your muscle memory, then that's what you're going to do.

Get Better Everyday

'Even if I have already peaked, I have to believe I can improve. I wake up every morning, and go to practice, with the illusion that I'm going to get better that day.' These words by Rafael Nadal give an insight into his grit and perseverance. And for anyone who's seen him play, this attitude is visible at every point he has played on the court.

Some of us just want to be great at what we do, while others enjoy the process of becoming better, no matter where they're at that moment. Practice is a space where you go in with humility. No matter how good you are, there's always room to grow and get better. Life around is evolving at a rapid pace, and it's on us to strive to keep up with it, and get better. We can't get to the top, and certainly can't stay there, if we don't stay sharp.

When it comes to practice though, it's not just about mindlessly stacking up the repetitions. Practice can seem fairly mundane, especially if we believe that it is meant to hone our skill alone. That's just one part of it. The true power of practice lies in how we can hone our mind. To win, no matter what.

Practice is an active effort. In fact, the effort that goes into practice should ideally be greater than the effort going into the final performance. This is because practice is where we get our hands dirty, it's where we come to terms with our weaknesses, confront our own limitations, and push ourselves to do better. In our quest for success, practice is where we face failure day after day.

Thus, each day you go into practice, set an intention. Think about what you want to achieve in that session. After practice, reflect on your experience. For some, writing about it helps too.

Practising Performance

When we practise, we often tend to practise our skills, not our performance. This is something that we often witness with students taking an examination. You may put in the hours studying, but may not always give enough importance to practising how to take the exam. After all, there's a lot more that goes into writing an exam than just knowing the answers. It's about how you deal with the pressure, how you pace yourself, and how you deal with the structure of the paper. Just one dress rehearsal isn't enough.

Working with a weightlifter once, we noticed that they performed a lot better in their first lift as compared to subsequent ones. On analyzing the situation further, we realized that the athlete felt a lot more nervous going into their subsequent lifts. Breaking it down, this anxiety was occurring due to the long timespan between their two lifts. During practice, the athlete was focusing simply on lifting their weights and getting in the right recovery. But this timespan was significantly shorter than what was taking place during competitions. In the time between two lifts, this player was observing others' performances and comparing them to their own, therefore the simple act of waiting for their own performance was leading to a lot of overthinking as well.

An example like this highlights simple, unsuspecting ways in which practice can be different from the actual performance. However, the solution is just as simple: prepare for the wait. Maintain a longer gap between two lifts, and ensure that you practise ways to keep yourself focused on your own performance rather than be distracted by others' scores.

Simulate Pressure

On a related note, it's not just the environmental conditions that we need to be prepared for. It's also important to recreate the pressure that we're likely to experience during our performance. This is where graded sample papers can be helpful, or practising interviews in front of other people rather than just in front of the mirror. In sport, this can take the form of setting stressful targets, like completing streaks or friendly matches.

When practising, we have a tendency to slightly slack off—missing the odd shot doesn't bother us. The problem here is that each time we use the wrong technique or play with lower intensity, it's not just an opportunity lost; it's a plus-one repetition added to the wrong technique. And these repetitions can really add up without us realizing. That's why it's critical that when you practise, approach every moment and point with the same seriousness, the same intensity and focus as you would on the final of a world cup.

Practice Imperfect

Now this can initially be a tough one to follow. You may be apprehensive; after all, aren't we always told to think positive and hope for the best? Hope for the best, yes. But we also have to prepare for the worst. And this is, in fact, a highly recommended strategy followed by elite athletes the world over.

We're going to take you back to Michael Phelps and the 2008 Olympic Games, where he went in with the mission to break the previous seven gold medals record set in 1972.

As he dove in for the 100 metre butterfly, his goggles filled with water and he couldn't see. Such an untoward incident would faze most players, but not Phelps. Why? Because he had prepared for it! He had practised swimming with his goggles filled with water, and when blinded, he reverted to his strategy of counting the number of strokes required to reach the end. This preparation was enough to get Michael that gold medal, and seven others as well.

What will you do if your equipment malfunctions? Or if you've lost time due to unforeseeable circumstances? Prepare for this in your practice. So, if you're preparing a dance performance, be prepared for the music to go off suddenly. Create that scenario in your training, and look at how you respond to the situation. Take the help of your coach, or even a friend, to create such scenarios.

Don't always train in ideal conditions, because that's not how the world works. Instead, practise with distractions. This is especially important for situations where we have only a select few shots—where maybe an event comes once every four years, or an exam which you can only take once a year. The idea is that if you've already prepared for everything that can go wrong, and, more importantly, created an action plan for it, then few things can faze you during your actual performance. As an added advantage, you'll also feel more confident and in control of the situation.

Practise Your Strengths

In our desire for perfection, we tend to focus on improving our weaknesses. While this is an essential aspect of training, we can't lose sight of what matters most—our strengths.

Your success depends on how well you capitalize on your strengths, so don't take them for granted.

Add Some Fun

If practice is repetitive and boring, you may end up dreading it, and subsequently avoiding it. Yes, it's important to get comfortable with the idea of boredom, since success comes with befriending repetition; however, that doesn't mean that practice has to be monotonous. Break down your practice sessions to train specific skills. Add innovative drills that challenge you. Put yourself in challenging situations, and figure solutions to get out of them. Keep learning new skills once the old ones become too easy. Consider gamifying your practice experience. Involve a peer in your training to bring in a social element as well. The idea is to make hard work enjoyable.

The Foundation for Confidence

Ask any athlete the secret behind their self-confidence, and their response is likely to be 'training'. If I've trained well, I'm going to play well. To beat everyone else in competition, I need to train harder than everybody else. There's simply no other way around it.

And, let's face it, we all know how much effort we actually put in. We can't lie to our own selves; the world out there shows us a mirror that we can't escape. So yes, self-talk can help, as can visualization, and several other strategies that we've spoken about. But in the absence of the training to back it, it's going to ring hollow.

Beware the Overtraining Syndrome

If you want to go out there and be a winner, you may feel that if you train longer hours than everyone else, you're going to outperform them all. At the same time, you have to ensure that you aren't pushing yourself too much. In sport, not giving yourself time to recover can lead to a phenomenon called overtraining syndrome. In the quest to be better than the rest, overtraining is actually detrimental to performance and increases risks of injury.

It's not very different in non-sport contexts. Recovery means both physical *and* mental, and the lack thereof can have a negative impact in any and every sphere of life. So make sure that you strike a balance. After all, over-tightening a guitar string doesn't make it sound better. It just makes it snap. The key is to strike the right balance.

Podium Finish

1. No matter the level you've reached, keep practising your skills.
2. Simulate real-life performance scenarios in your practice.
3. Practise with focus. Practise with intention.

Do you often find yourself stuck behind the curve? Can predicting what comes next help you?

7

A Step Ahead: Developing Anticipation

'I skate to where the puck is going to be, not where it's been.'

—Wayne Gretzky

As professionals caught up in high-pressure environments, we often find ourselves living from crisis to crisis. Be it heaps of paperwork, team conflicts or solving operational problems, we get blindsided by what life throws at us and invest all our time *reacting* to situations, as they seem to just come at us from out of nowhere! We stay trapped in this cycle time and again. Rarely are we able to really take charge of our own destiny and forge our own path ahead.

There are a few people, however, who remain unfazed as new challenges unfold; who seem to have an uncanny knack of being able to predict and being prepared for the most challenging of situations, even before anyone else gets a whiff of it.

It's the same way on the sport field as well. While most of us scramble to read the pitch, break defence and reach the ball, there are a few chosen players who make it seem so effortless. You end up wondering—do they have eyes at the back of their heads? Are they mind readers? Fortune tellers? Or does life simply unfold in slow-mo just for them?

A New Insight

Sport scientists have always been eager to identify what it is that separates the elite players from amateurs—the X factor that turns some players into superstars. And this opportunity arrived when they studied Cristiano Ronaldo and what it took for him to tackle seemingly impossible situations.

The design of the study was straightforward: receive the ball from a corner kick and hit it into the goal. There was just a simple complication—the lights would be turned off the moment the other player kicked the ball towards Ronaldo. Can you fathom even making contact with a ball you cannot see, let alone receiving it and hitting it into a goal that is basically invisible at that moment?

Other players who attempted this challenge were obviously dumbfounded. The ball flew light years away from them. However, things were different with Ronaldo. He received the ball, hit it into the back of the net, and made it all look really easy at the same time.

Lights out!

Everyone says 'keep your eye on the ball'. But what happens when the lights are turned off? Well, what Ronaldo did was he captured all the information he could before the lights went out. He focused on the posture of the player passing the ball, where was he looking, which way his feet were pointing, the weight balance of his hips, and the loudness of the sound at impact—once all these factors had been taken into account, being able to see the ball was just not important enough anymore. In fact, elite athletes often train with vision-occlusion glasses so that their minds get into the habit of filling in the blanks.

The Power of Pattern Recognition

We understand that experts have better skills than novices; they're able to execute a move better than others. But look up close and you'll realize that it's not just their execution skill that's better; it's also their perceptual skills. Experts are able to recognize patterns, and therefore catch signals from the environment faster than novices can. Remember the butterfly effect? Events in the world are deeply interconnected, even if those connections aren't always clear for us to see. The more you practise recognizing patterns in your sphere of work, the larger that web of connections becomes for you.

Remember that the cues are out there for all of us to see. Whatever the field of work may be, there will always be indicators that help us foresee what comes next. All you need to do is know where to look for them.

Practise Anticipation

It's not about being sentient, it's about training and practice. Chess players do it all the time. While beginner chess players can see up to two or three moves in advance (that too, forced moves), grandmasters are able to see several probable outcomes ahead. Magnus Carlsen claims that he can see 15, sometimes up to 20, moves ahead in his mind! That too, keeping in mind all the different ways in which his opponent may respond to each of those moves. Chess players also often practise with their eyes closed, so they're able to hone their ability to strategize through visualization, rather than relying on the placement of pieces on the actual chessboard.

Be Aware of Your Surroundings

The building block of this kind of ninja ability to accurately predict events is to become situationally aware—just be aware of things around you. Sounds pretty basic, right? Let's try a simple test. Close your eyes and think back to your place of work. Visualize every detail—whether it's the stationery on your desk or the memories pinned on your board. How vividly can you recreate the entire picture?

The idea behind this test is to reflect on how much of our environment we really take in. For a civilization that has its nose buried in smartphones and ears covered with blaring headphones, it's not something that comes naturally to us. Not anymore at least. The first step then is to just observe. Start simple. Unplug yourself from all your devices for half an hour each day and just take the time to look around you. You can do this while travelling to work, going for a walk, sitting at a coffee shop, or even when just relaxing at home. Notice the sights, sounds and smells. Don't be passive, lost in your own thoughts. Observation is an active process that requires you to be present and alert. So engage with your environment.

See if you recognize any patterns in your environment. Form basic hypotheses, and test whether they come true. Read between the lines. Be curious, be interested!

Use All Your Senses

When we talk about observation, it's usually regarding the things we can see with our eyes. In going about our everyday lives, we tend to rely most heavily on our sense of sight, but the truth is that each of our senses plays a key role in how we perceive our environment, and how we experience a moment. The music we hear has the power to uplift our mood or take us to the depths of despair; familiar smells can trigger feelings of joy, disgust and nostalgia.

We can gather so much more information from our environment if we allow ourselves to utilize all of our senses. Once more, this improves the ability to recognize patterns and predict outcomes. So, experience every moment to the fullest by engaging all your senses—not only will it help you stay calmer and more grounded in the present moment, but also actually help you make more effective and informed decisions.

Look at the Bigger Picture

To focus doesn't mean staying endlessly fixated on the ball. Instead, it's time to view your focus as a lens that can zoom in and pan out at will. To be on top of things requires flexibility in focus, zooming in and out of immediate challenges as well as the larger context in which we are operating. While in moments of crises this might sound next to impossible, some simple practices can actually go a long way. For starters, make it a habit that no matter how hectic your schedule may be, you take out a few minutes to step back from the situation. Spend 15 minutes in quiet contemplation. You don't need an agenda for how to use this time—use it as a moment to disengage from the immediate situation, and as an opportunity to introspect and reflect on the bigger picture.

Read! Read not just about your field of work, but just about everything you can get your hands on. In fact, be it a newspaper or a novel, the more you read, the more you'll gain a better understanding of how the world works, and how people think and operate. Expose yourself to different ways of thinking. Watch new, diverse things; talk to people with different experiences, perspectives and worldviews.

It's also a good idea to talk through your strategy. Several times, after an event, we believe we could have predicted the outcome. This is known in social psychology as the 'hindsight bias', and hindsight is 20/20. Engaging in such conversations after the event is not going to help us. Instead, be proactive. As an event is taking place, develop the practice of verbalizing your understanding. Share it with someone who is more experienced in the field, and let them become a sounding board for you. Avoid rueful post-mortems. Instead, practise this in real time so you're able to actually see (and perhaps predict) the big picture unfold, and take steps towards managing it.

Look One Step Ahead

When a ball approaches you at speeds of over 160 kmph, there's simply no way you can see the ball, evaluate the flight and make a decision. The only way you can really play this ball is by looking at field placements, evaluating previous deliveries, and looking at the fingers of the bowler.

So, don't wait for problems to arise to take decisions. Be aware of everything going on in the larger context. Start reading the body language of others around you. Be mindful of patterns and trends. Take a bird's-eye view of the field to understand the wheels and cogs, and be mindful of the seemingly distant developments that have an impact on us in the here and now. Make an informed decision; execute.

As you set out on your path to develop this Ronaldo-esque foresight, remember that anticipation is not a skill that comes overnight, or even a skill that comes to us automatically. It requires us to make a deliberate change from our usual ways of living. It requires a fair amount of trial and error. And, most of all, it requires lots and lots of practice.

As Gretzky said, 'Do it once and it's an exercise. Do it a few thousand times and it's "uncanny anticipation".'

Podium Finish

1. Anticipation is a skill, not a gift. Hone it.
2. Become aware of your surroundings. Learn to observe life as it unfolds around you.
3. Look at the bigger picture. Recognize patterns.

What is the one thing you say to yourself in difficult moments?

8

The Coach Within: Mastering Self-Talk

'You have to stay relaxed and keep your mind clear. I would tell myself to take it one point at a time, no matter the situation.'

—Pete Sampras

Pete Sampras has often been hailed for his incredible mental toughness and focus on the court. He's also famous for using self-talk to manage pressure, stay confident, and deal with the challenges that one must surmount to become a Grand Slam champion.

Interestingly, Andre Agassi, a contemporary of Pete Sampras, famously wrote in his book *Open*, 'Tennis is the sport in which you talk to yourself...tennis is so damned lonely...the rules forbid a tennis player from even talking to his coach while on the court...you're on an island...'

It's not just about tennis though. Out there, on the big stage, it can get lonely. You don't always have a team as your support system during those crunch moments. It's just you.

Nobody is there to calm you down, reassure you, or tell you what to do. And this is where self-talk is key. For everything that you've been taught by your teachers, your family, your support system—self-talk holds the key to unlocking these learnings, and to using them at a time when it matters most. Self-talk is the coach within: the answer to staying motivated, building confidence, maintaining focus, managing emotions, and even following the right technique.

A Window into the Self

The person we talk to the most during the day is our own self. And because we're so used to the chatter going on in our minds, we treat it like second nature. We don't often stop to question it, see how it impacts our everyday life, and whether it serves to help or hinder us in our pursuits.

View your self-talk from a distance, and you'll see it's like getting to know the Central Command System of your mind. You may not realize it, but it's this self-talk that colours our every perception and action. It's what determines how motivated we feel, where we choose to focus, how we manage our emotions, how we deal with setbacks, and just every aspect of our personality. Our self-talk is, in its essence, a window into our most deeply held beliefs. Listen closely to your self-talk, and you'll get to know what you really feel, about yourself, others, and your past, present and future.

The Goals We Set

We've spoken about setting the right kind of goals in a previous chapter, but beyond the contents of our goals, *how* we phrase them also matters. It matters a lot, in fact. When we talk of self-talk, we need to deep-dive into the exact nature of the words we use, and their tonality as well. Consider the two statements, 'I *want* to win' and 'I *have* to win'. Seems like a fairly minor distinction, sure. But the impact that each of these statements have are worlds apart. Using the phrase 'want to' reflects a desire to achieve. The phrase 'have to', on the other hand, has several connotations attached to it. Beyond the desire to win, could it perhaps reflect an underlying pressure from one's own self or another? A statement like this begs the question, 'what will happen if you don't win?' And then, an enjoyable challenge suddenly turns into a threatening situation with lots to lose. It's the same with words like 'should', which reflect deep-rooted societal expectations and pressures. We *should* win because it's what's 'right' or what's expected of us—then not achieving it may bring about feelings of guilt or even shame. If you find yourself using phrases like 'I must', 'I have to', or 'I should', take a moment to introspect. Ask yourself what these pressures are.

After all, our goals shouldn't frighten or terrorize us. Their role is to guide us, excite us, and motivate us.

Recognize the Chatter

Close your eyes for a minute and try to notice what goes on in your mind. It's likely that you'll notice a barrage of thoughts and images flowing through your mind. Some may excite you, some may worry you, others may make you reminisce about the past. Either way, you'll notice that there's plenty that you weren't actively thinking of that has suddenly 'popped' into your mind.

Many times, we confuse this mindless chatter with our self-talk. We believe that all of the random thoughts that come into our mind must really be who we are. So when I hear an alarm go off, my first thought may be, 'oh, I don't want to wake up and go to work today.' This is the first instinctive, unthinking thought that comes into our mind. Yet, there is another part of the mind: the Central Command System. The one that can say, 'how does it matter, let's just sleep in,' or 'ok, time to wake up and get ready for work.' This is our real self-talk. Self-talk is not about passively listening to our thoughts; it's about actively speaking to ourselves. This is what determines what choices we make and the person we are.

So when your thoughts are having their own little party in your mind, don't be disheartened or get carried away. These thoughts are like a radio playing in the background. They don't have the power to determine how we really behave. Recognize that the choice to act is still yours, and here's where you use the power of self-talk to make choices that really matter.

The Coach Within

Success is not just about the right attitude, but about the right technique as well. While preparing, we often focus on our technique, but during high-pressure performance situations, this focus often shifts from the technique to managing our own emotions and the noise that accompanies significant events. And this is where you need the coach within to kick into action—to bring the focus back to what's really important.

Use your self-talk to give yourself specific instructions. In the case of tennis, for example, this could mean keeping the racket low, being agile with the footwork. It could be a reminder to focus on a particular strategy or maintain the right body language.

Cue words are a particularly helpful strategy within self-talk. It's not always possible to give ourselves long sermons, which can be time-consuming and even distracting. The idea is to keep things as simple as possible. Associating simple words or phrases with an action pattern is a technique used by several elite athletes. For instance, just saying the word 'go' can serve as a trigger for you to launch the ball up in the air and give your body the cue to feel energized and move in its most natural, automatic and practised manner. It's the same before starting a performance recital, a presentation, or writing an exam.

Like every other skill, remember that self-talk works if we practise it. Cue words won't work if we only use them during crunch moments. It's during the preparation phase that we need to pair the self-talk with the actions, so that one serves as a reminder for the other. In this way, our self-talk and actions work seamlessly in tandem.

Keep It Positive

Yes, we've all heard that we should think positive, and say positive things to ourselves. But what does that really mean? And, more importantly, does it really work?

What we're talking about here is not the power of affirmations. Instead, we're talking about using self-talk in a simple, instructional way that helps us achieve our targets in an efficient manner. And to do this, the first thing we need to know is that our mind is like a toddler—it doesn't understand *no* very well. So, if we tell you to *not* think about a pink elephant, guess what! We can safely assume there's a pink elephant swirling about in your mind at this moment.

Now, let's put this in the context of a task you have to do. Every time we repeat to ourselves, 'Don't hit outside the line, don't hit outside the line,' inadvertently our focus shifts to 'outside the line'. It may even shift our gaze outside the line without our knowing. And every time we say this statement, our mind does a mental rehearsal of 'outside the line, outside the line'. The result is that we end up doing exactly what we don't want to, which thus impacts our belief in our own self. Why couldn't we follow something so simple? Well, the mind did follow it; it's just that it was the wrong command to give.

Understanding this, it's now important to phrase our self-talk in a way that is precise and instructive. Let's tell our mind what we want it to do, not what we don't want it to do. 'Hit the shot six inches inside the line,' for example, is positively phrased; it's precise, and it's the only thing that our mind will now focus on.

You Got This

Before Simone Biles jumped onto the balance beam to attempt one of the most difficult manoeuvres at the Paris 2024 Olympics, she said three words to herself: You got this.

When things get tough, it's not unusual for the chatter to kick in, and for the mind to want to give up. We start making excuses or even questioning the point of continuing at all.

It's here once more that our self-talk comes to the rescue. Keep talking to yourself, whether in your mind or, frankly, even out loud. Use it to drown out the self-doubt. Remind yourself of why you're there and of the efforts that you've put into being where you are. Tell yourself to keep going, that you've trained for this day, that you've got this! When things get tough, be your own cheerleader.

> **Podium Finish**
>
> 1. Self-talk is your inner coach. Know what you need to tell yourself and when.
> 2. Be deliberate, be constructive, and be positive.
> 3. Don't be a passive listener. Recognize and control the chatter.

Take a minute to list all the
things that distract you.

9

Quiet Eye: The Science of Focus

'If you can keep playing tennis when someone is shooting a gun down the street, that's concentration.'

—Serena Williams

In the world of performance, attention is famously referred to as the currency of success. Yet, ironically, we're all so profligate with how we spend this currency. Surrounded by our gadgets, we're plagued by distractions every waking moment. In fact, even our sleep isn't spared anymore.

We often speak about how difficult we find it to focus. Yet, how many of us go out of our way to train our focus? Tiger Woods' father and coach, Earl Woods, did just this. He didn't just teach his son how to swing the club, he taught him how to play in the real world. As Tiger was training, Earl went out of his way to distract him. He dropped clubs, made noises, moved around in his line of vision, and even involved other family members to distract him with their activities.

The Nature of Distractions

Distractions are all around us, vying for our limited attention span. Some distractions are easy to identify, like the noise in our environment that doesn't allow us to focus. But many times, distractions come disguised. They masquerade as things that seem urgent and must be attended to right away. The most common example of this is a social media notification popping up that we feel compelled to open, respond to, or delete at the very least.

These distractions exist both in our external and internal environment. Internally, these can take the form of pain or an emotion that overwhelms us. The most common distraction though is our own thoughts! And because these thoughts are so ubiquitous, and we're so used to living with them, we don't often recognize how distracting they really can be.

How then do we recognize what is a distraction and what isn't? What shall we then focus on? We focus on what is useful. After all, just because something is true doesn't mean that it's important. Anything that takes us away from our goal is a distraction. Or rather, anything that doesn't help achieve what we've set out to do is a distraction. So, if we're so afraid of an exam result that we end up not studying for it, then that fear is a distraction. Another version of this is thought 'what if I fail?', or any prediction about the results of our exam.

The Spotlight

People often speak about difficulty in focusing. Think about it though: is it possible to ever stop focusing? Not really.

Every distraction is basically focus shifted elsewhere. Let's rephrase the problem statement then. The difficulty is in focusing on what we want to focus on, rather than our focus shifting to things that are less important.

To understand focus, it's helpful to think of it as a spotlight. This spotlight doesn't switch on and off; instead, it merely shifts. It can shift to stage left or right, depending on the character that needs to be highlighted. It can be a narrow beam or light up a broad area, depending on the perspective you're looking for.

Recognize that your focus is flexible and learn to shift it around at your own will. Try this simple exercise, which will take just about three minutes. For one minute, focus on all the sounds around you. In the second minute, notice the different colours you can see in your environment. In the third minute, close your eyes and focus on your breathing.

You'll notice that when you're focusing on the sounds, you're not really aware of your breathing. Or when your eyes are scanning for the colours in your surroundings, the sounds simply settle into white noise in the background. Practise versions of this drill to train your mind, so you can bring the spotlight under your own control.

Ctrl + F

Speaking of control, take a moment to notice the things you focus on. How often do you find yourself complaining about the weather, or the traffic on the road? How often do you fret about timelines and wish they were different? How much does your focus shift to other people and their responses? How often do you get carried away by a referee's call you don't agree with? Most of all, how often do you daydream about getting a certain kind of result?

The one thing all of these questions have in common is that they're all out of your sphere of control. And yet, notice how much time you spend talking about these things. When it comes to any life situation, there are some things that are in our control, and many more that aren't. Most of our stress in life comes from focusing all our energy on worrying about things that we can't control.

So the first thing to do to bring our focus in our control is to focus on the controllables. Ignore things that you can't influence, no matter how important they seem. They are, at the end of the day, distractions.

Here and Now

Think about why very simple catches sometimes get dropped. You see the ball coming your way, you get excited that you're going to catch it, and your mind shifts to the celebrations that will take place after you catch the ball. However, you lose focus on the ball and end up dropping a simple shot. It's what happens most often when people speak of unforced errors or 'silly mistakes'.

Another way to think about distractions is to notice things that take you away from the present moment, the here and now. If you make a mistake and are worried about how your coach will react, then recognize that your focus has shifted from the present moment to the future. Now to then. It's also shifted from the court to the locker room. Here to there.

It's the same with results. While preparing or performing, results are never in the now. They're always in the future. In fact, you'll also notice that the scoreboard is never placed inside the playing zone; it's always outside the court. Each time you notice your focus shifting from the present moment, bring it back to what matters. Here. Now.

Look Out to Focus

The most effective way to bring your focus to the here and now is to focus on the environment around you. Might sound a bit counter-intuitive, but it makes sense when we think about the extent to which our thoughts and emotions distract us.

As we have discussed in previous chapters, the reason most of us choke under pressure is actually a change in our focus. We become more self-conscious rather than task-focused. We start overthinking things that we already know how to do—very well, we may add. Unfortunately, in overthinking and over-controlling it, we end up making mistakes. We tend to do this even more in high-stress situations, where we feel that the stakes are too high. Our focus shifts to managing our internal state rather than the real task at hand.

An internal focus, i.e. focusing on our own thoughts or body, works when we're strategizing or preparing ourselves physically. But when it's time to execute, the focus has to be outwards. As an example, a batter has to focus all their attention on the ball coming their way rather than on their own grip, footwork or the angle of their bat.

Interestingly, there have been comparative studies conducted on novice and expert players across various sports, and researchers have found a significant difference in this very zone of focus that we're talking about. While novice golfers focus on their swing or the angle of their clubs, expert golfers focus on the flag or wherever they want to hit the ball. Try this experiment yourself—if you want to jump as high as you can, make one attempt where you focus on the explosive push from your legs. Make the second attempt where your focus is simply on touching the ceiling, and let your body work however it does. Chances are your second jump will be higher.

This strategy is very effective when it comes to any automatic task. Use it in places where you've practised your skill several times and can now use it without putting much conscious thought into it.

Another place to practise this is during exercise. If you want to increase your stamina while running, don't focus on your heart rate or your legs hitting the ground. You're going to feel more tired. Instead, watch the scenery around you or listen to some music. When the focus is not on your heartbeat, you'll find yourself running longer distances and feeling less tired. It's all a game of perception.

The Right Commands

Given how prone our mind is to distractions, giving it the right commands becomes essential. Like we've spoken about in previous chapters, if we say 'don't think about chocolate ice cream,' you're going to be thinking about chocolate ice cream, whether you like it or not. You're also going to picture it and may start drooling as a result! Ideas that were never in your mind are there now. That's the power of self-suggestions. So, to train your mind to stay away from distractions, make your commands specific and positive. Only feed your mind what you want it to focus on, not what you want it to avoid.

Power of the Quiet Eye

When it comes to sport, there's been much research conducted to identify what separates the best from the rest. Aside from the external focus that expert athletes utilize, researchers have identified another aspect of visual-motor behaviour that separates them from the novices. It's called 'quiet eye'. Essentially, they found that just before executing a task, expert athletes tend to linger their gaze at one spot longer. Novices, on the other hand, shift their gaze from one aspect of the field to the other.

One might think that flitting our gaze from one aspect to another is useful in gathering a lot of environmental data, but peak performance is actually about quietening the mind—and quietening the eye is one pathway to do just this. Letting your gaze linger a few seconds longer and keeping it steady slows down the mind's cognitive activity, which is otherwise heightened, especially during stressful situations. Quiet eye can then enhance your visual perception, help you gather and synthesize more data from the environment, enable you to make better decisions, and most of all, prevent you from choking during crucial moments in your performance.

Building the Focus Muscle

Like everything else we've spoken about in this book, focus is a skill. And all skills can be learnt and mastered through practice. Time and again, we train ourselves on our technique and content. Nevertheless, we aren't that meticulous about training these all-important mental skills. We hope that these skills will simply kick in when we need them, but nothing could be further from the truth. We need to train our focus during practice so that it comes to our aid during real-life crunch moments.

Think of building focus like building muscle; the first few repetitions are more of a warm-up. The muscle is actually built during the last repetitions, the ones where you feel the burn. Similarly, with focus, you'll only build it when you put in the repetitions. And what better way to build our focus muscle than to sustain it even when we're bored, tired or annoyed.

A simple exercise to build focus is to just sit quietly and focus on your breathing. As your thoughts distract you, learn to recognize your mind wandering and bring it back each time. Start off slow, maybe just two to three minutes, then gradually build up the time. Remember to challenge yourself if you want to build that focus muscle. Another exercise is the focus ladder. Count 1–10, each time accompanied by a long inhalation and long exhalation. Breathe in...breathe out...one...and so on. Once you reach 10, count back 10–1. Do this multiple times within a set time limit. If your thoughts wander and you lose count, start over from one again. Again, it might seem boring, but that's kind of the point.

Listening to a piece of music and following one particular instrument, solving puzzles like crosswords, Sudoku and jigsaws are other fun ways in which you can build your focus. Just remember not to leave it when it gets difficult or boring.

Another point to keep in mind here is that many times when we're trying to build our focus, we try to create an ideal environment. We often notice people do breathwork or visualizations in a very quiet, conducive environment. On the other hand, though, being able to build focus in the midst of distractions is likely to be more effective. So, don't wait for the perfect environment; practise your focus drills wherever you are.

In fact, it's also a good idea to include distractions as part of your practice sessions. If you're preparing for a presentation, don't insulate yourself entirely. You may get annoyed by someone else speaking in the background, but then that's life, and such situations may arise wherever you are.

Have Some Serious Fun!

What does fun have to do with focus? Turns out, everything! We've already described a lot of drills that you can practise to enhance your focus, but the one simplest, most efficient way of staying focused is actually just having fun.

Think about the last time you had fun. It could be dancing to your favourite songs, chatting with your friends, playing a sport, or working on a puzzle. Now notice how focused you were during that time. Were you thinking about what other people were thinking? What you were going to eat for breakfast the next day? About a presentation that went badly the previous week? Probably not! If you're having fun, you're not in the past or the future. Fun is about being in the moment, in the here and now.

Having fun doesn't mean you're not taking the activity seriously. On the contrary, you can only truly enjoy an activity if you're completely absorbed in it. Whatever it is you're doing at this moment is the only thing that matters. Some people have also referred to this feeling as one of 'flow', where you're in the moment, and your mind and body are seamlessly connected. Peak performance doesn't have to be all about repetitions and pushing yourself to the limit. It also has to do with enjoying what you're doing. It's easier to think about this in the context of sport where you're enjoying playing, but this is actually true for just about any activity. So next time you're working on a deadline, enjoy it. Whether it's a debate or a negotiation, a competition or a workout, have fun while you do it. The focus will follow you effortlessly.

Creating Reality

At the end of the day, remember that focus is the light that's in our control. Where we shed light becomes our reality, and darkness turns to oblivion. So hone this skill and use it wisely. In the words of Qui Gon from *Star Wars*, 'Always remember, your focus determines your reality.'

> **Podium Finish**
>
> 1. Distractions are everywhere—within us and beyond.
> 2. The present moment is what matters the most. Here and now.
> 3. Fun fuels focus.

What is your image of success?

10

Seeing is Believing: Visualization for Performance

'Visualization combines concentration, imagination and belief. Concentration is the ability to think about a single thing or task without internal or external interruption; imagination is the creative ability to see yourself in a wide range of situations and envision how you'd navigate them; belief is unshakable confidence in your own abilities. These qualities are crucial to success in sports.'

—Kobe Bryant

Swimming is an event where the difference between first and second place is often a fraction of a second. But for Katie Ledecky in the 2016 Rio Olympics, this gap was over 20 seconds. Even now, as you watch the replay, all you can see is Ledecky and the world record line in the frame. There's no other competitor to be seen. And mind you, all this while, Ledecky is in the pool with seven others of the fastest female swimmers in the world. When asked about her preparation in an interview, Ledecky said, 'I have my goals, and I visualize things to help me achieve those goals. So just different ways I swim my races, how my stroke needs to feel...what my strokes should feel like at different parts of the race, and I can just kind of picture that in my mind...' Michael Phelps too has spoken about visualization, describing it as running his 'mental videotape'.

A Way of Thinking

Whether it's an upcoming board meeting or the D-Day of a long-planned project, our mind is abound with all kinds of scenarios that may emerge. We may dread the deathly silence of the crowd, look forward to a pat on the back by a senior colleague, or fret about the entire show falling to pieces.

Good or bad, take a moment to think about how it is that you process these scenarios. Is it just the words that play out as thoughts? Quite the contrary. When we look at future situations, that's exactly what we do—we *look* at them. They play out like scenes before us where we can see everybody's expressions, hear the words, and physically feel the tension.

And that brings us to visualization—thinking through images. Words enter our mind one by one and can slow us down. Images, instead, appear in a flash, accumulating thousands of bits of information in an instant. This is what makes visualization one of our most primitive, and most powerful, methods of learning, practising and processing information.

Visualization for Boosting Confidence

If life was a cricket match and you were declared player of the match, what would your highlights film at the end of the game look like? Think back to the ups and downs you've experienced, the challenges you've faced, the wins you've had, the odds you've defied.

Now create a two-minute film in your mind of your three greatest moments of success—your personal highlights movie. When you make this collection, don't just focus on the winning moment, relive how you got there. Imagining results alone isn't enough; for visualization to be effective, you need to delve into the process of how you got there. So, picture the effort you invested, the courage you showed, the strength you felt, and the people who stood by you through it all. Feel yourself standing tall and victorious, and let the confidence surge through your system.

We can't stress this enough. The belief that you can succeed is actually a crucial factor in determining actual success. A kind of self-fulfilling prophecy, this belief in yourself encourages you to work harder, expend more energy, deal with stress more effectively, and persist in the face of hardships—all of which are more likely to lead to a successful outcome.

Make sure that you have this two-minute mental video clip ready in your toolbox. When things seem difficult, draw from past successes to stay confident. Replay the movie every morning before you go to work, every time you're entering a high-powered meeting, every time you have a difficult task at hand, and most importantly, every time you suspect self-doubt creeping in.

Visualization for Relaxation

When the stress overwhelms us, we often find it difficult to concentrate. Often, our mind is tempted to avoid the present situation and instead takes a flight into fantasy. Unfortunately, most of the times, this just leads to us ruminating about past disappointments. Or worse, we end up imagining scenarios of failure in the future. Lost in this unhelpful reverie, neither are we able to deal with the situation at hand, nor are we able to ease the distress that comes along with it. But what if we could turn this unhelpful rumination into a deliberate 'mental vacation'?

Imagine a place that is perfect; a place that calms you down and brings you joy. It could be standing on a mountain top, walking through a forest, or sitting on a beach watching the waves gushing in. It could be a place you have already been to or a place you've always imagined or dreamed of.

A happy place isn't just something you see, it's something you must experience. For your imagination to work its magic, immerse yourself in this experience with all your senses. If you're imagining yourself walking through the forest, listen to the birds chirp and the leaves rustle. Watch the golden sunlight breaking through the trees and warm your skin. Smell the fresh air, and feel the oxygen fill your lungs. Feel the earth beneath your feet with every step you take. Take a few minutes to walk along, exploring this area—you don't need to rush yourself. As you enter a clearing, you may stumble upon a quiet blue lake with crystal-clear waters. Feel the cool water as you dip your feet in, watch the ripples in the water, and hear the 'plop' as a pebble falls in. Stay in the moment. Breathe in the tranquillity. Bring yourself back to the present once you feel ready.

It's true that escaping to your happy place can't solve your problems—you will still have to come back and face the situation at hand. But what it does do is provide a much-needed mental break. It breaks the cycle of worry and stops the body's stress response. In fact, it can be so effective that once you get comfortable with it, it can actually result in changes in heart rate, respiration and blood pressure. It can decrease perceptions of pain, help you sleep better at night, and even boost immunity.

Visualization for Building Skill

There's no doubt that imagery can influence our emotions by activating our autonomic nervous system. But the power of imagery isn't restricted to making you feel better. In fact, its most prominent use in the field of sport is to help athletes enhance their technical skills and learn plays faster.

Over the last few years, there's been a lot of research on how powerful imagery can really be, and the results have been promising. There's been some fascinating research that has found that imaginary exercise activates the same areas of the brain as real exercise, and can actually even increase muscle strength! Of course, the gains aren't comparable to those of real exercise, but they've been found to be present nonetheless.

Now, keep in mind that the idea behind sharing this information isn't to turn you into a couch potato. Mental training can complement physical training, not really substitute it. For skill development, imagery works best if we actually not just see but feel ourselves performing an activity; a technique more specifically known as motor imagery. This can be particularly effective if, for instance, you're looking to learn a new instrument. Close your eyes and visualize playing the instrument. Don't just see it, feel it. This requires you to become aware of your body movements, and even feel the muscles as they tense and contract while you perform a task. In this method, mental imagery can engage not just the senses but even the motor system involved in executing skills. In this way, carrying out the entire procedure time and again, with sufficient repetition, works in two ways. It exercises relevant areas of the brain. At the same time, it builds associations amongst the different processes required to interact with one another to facilitate a more complex performance.

Just keep in mind that the pace of this imagery is in your control. You can slow it down or crank it up as per your skill level. Like with real practice, it might be a good idea to start in slow motion to ensure greater accuracy, but make sure to bring it up to real-time speed by the end for a more realistic experience.

Imagery to Prepare for the Big Day

> Part of my preparation is I go and ask the kit man what colour we're wearing—if it's red top, white shorts, white socks or black socks... Then I lie in bed the night before the game and visualize myself scoring goals or doing well. You're trying to put yourself in that moment and trying to prepare yourself, to have a 'memory' before the game. I don't know if you'd call it visualizing or dreaming, but I've always done it, my whole life.

Seeing is Believing: Visualization for Performance

These are the words of Wayne Rooney, the prolific English footballer, shared when he was asked how he prepared for his matches.

Whether it's a football match or a big company event, visualization can help you prepare for everything. Use this technique to run through the entire event—visualize the ideal execution, but also take a moment to plan for all that might go wrong. The idea here isn't to start worrying but instead to form easy-access contingency plans if things go south. Visualize everything from the clothes you will wear, to your posture and body language, and how you will handle difficult questions that may be asked of you. Take a few moments the night before to do this mental planning and groundwork. Doing so will help you feel more prepared, more in control, and more confident as you step into the biggest moments of your life.

Podium Finish

1. It's not magic. Visualization is a skill that you can use to enhance your performance.
2. Use visualization to relax, feel confident and practise your skills.
3. Use all your senses. The more realistic the image, the better.

Can you think of a memory when fear has helped you perform better?

11

Fight, Flight or Freeze: Embracing the Adrenaline Rush

'Fear is just like fire, it can be helpful if you know how to use it. If not, you'll get burned.'

—Mike Tyson

How would you feel if you were asked to stand on a platform the size of a pizza box, 40 feet above the ground? Well, that is exactly what Abhinav Bindra did, as part of his preparation for the 2008 Olympic Games, which won him his historic gold medal in Beijing. It's something that was practised by the German military as part of their training, which is where Bindra was in the lead-up to the Games.

When asked about his experience of climbing the pizza box pole, he said that halfway up the climb he had decided he couldn't go on. Even though he was hooked on to safety wires, he felt afraid.

When we think of shooting, we think of calmness and

stillness. We don't automatically associate it with physical prowess. Why then was Bindra doing German military drills? Why was he climbing up a pole to a pizza box to prepare to shoot? He was doing it to conquer fear—the same fear that would grip him in the Olympic finals. And that's why he pushed on and finally stood trembling at the top.

As a sport psychologist, when one thinks of competitive pressure, the sport that first comes to mind is shooting. Shooting as a sport may seem pretty mundane, even boring to watch to the outside spectator. But get inside the heart and mind of a shooter, and you come to realize the intense internal battle that rages. It's not a competition with other players; the opponent is your own self.

Imagine this: the distance between the rifle and the target is 10 metres, and the target is just 0.5 millimetre. The winner is decided by the tiniest fraction of a millimetre. The precision required is such that the shooters must learn to shoot *between* heartbeats—even the disruption caused by a heartbeat is enough to throw the shooter off target.

The Pressures of Performance

On the other hand, the pressure keeps mounting. As thousands of spectators look on, an endless stream of negative thoughts run through your mind. 'What if I lose?', 'What will people watching me say?', 'This is the most important moment of my life, nothing can go wrong!', and so on. With it comes the barrage of fight or flight responses, your heart starts pounding, your breath quickens, your muscles tense up, you get butterflies in your stomach, and you break out into a sweat.

This is not an experience unique to shooting or to sport. We're all bound to have experienced it at several points in our lives. Ever broken into sweat while making an important presentation? Ever noticed your heart beating faster when waiting outside your boss's cabin? Ever felt so overwhelmed that your hands started trembling as you signed a document or even just held a glass? From preparing for an exam to appearing in an interview, making a presentation, performing on stage, going out on a date, and several more, this stress response visits us time and again.

Understanding the Fight-Flight Response

When faced with imminent danger, our mind has three default ways of responding. We may choose to confront the threat (fight), run away from it (flight), or sometimes just be completely immobilized (freeze).

Each of these responses are in fact physiological reactions—rather, they are a chain of rapidly occurring reactions inside the body. Why does our body behave in such unhelpful ways in the face of stress? Well, these mechanisms didn't start out as being unhelpful and counterproductive. To understand the stress response in its entirety, we need to look at it from an evolutionary perspective. At a time in human history when our ancestors were hunter-gatherers, the threats they encountered were from wild animals, natural disasters, or aggressive tribes competing for resources. Each of these required us to respond with a burst of physical strength. It could have been in the form of fighting against other tribes (fight), running away from a wild animal (flight), or sometimes staying completely still, like when confronted by a venomous snake (freeze).

And so, the stress response was our body's way of energizing us, to become stronger as we faced these threats—a turbo boost of adrenaline, if you will. The heart beat faster and breathing quickened to increase oxygen supply to the limbs. The pupils dilated to allow more light to come in, blood rushed to the extremities of our body, and the muscles clenched in preparation for a fight. When you look at stress this way, you realize that stress was never meant to be a weakness. In fact, it was quite the opposite!

We all speak of fear as a hindrance, but there's a flip side to this fear. It's this fear that gets the heart pumping more blood to reach the muscles; it's this fear that leads us to breathe in more oxygen; it's this fear that dilates the pupils to let in more light. Fear gives the body the strength, the energy and the alertness to defy the greatest odds. Without this 'fear', there probably would be no real success either.

Accept the Stress

There's probably nothing more frustrating than when someone says 'just relax' when you're nervous or stressed. We surely would if we could. But certain events are going to get the adrenaline rushing through you, whether you like it or not. Playing for the country is obviously a lot more nerve-wracking than playing street cricket, just like making a big presentation is more anxiety-provoking than talking amongst friends.

Stress is not necessarily a bad thing; it's actually simply your body's inbuilt response to energize you to cope with immediate threats. These responses have always been a part of our DNA—the only problem is they were meant for creature threats like snakes and tigers. In the modern-day world, these tigers have been replaced by presentations, social evaluations, exams, deadlines and unrelenting bosses.

The way you're feeling isn't 'wrong', so don't wrestle with the rush that comes from confronting testing situations. In fact, telling an anxious person to relax can actually increase their anxiety! It makes one feel bad about feeling anxious, like it's somehow their fault or a personal weakness they can't control.

When athletes speak about their goals for a competition, they often cite, 'I just want to be relaxed in the competition.' Now the player may think that what they're setting is a process goal that's in their control. But because it's so difficult to regulate our internal state, and because feeling anxious in evaluative situations is normal, feeling stressed may make them feel like they've failed at something they believed to be simple and straightforward. Hyper-focusing on trying to relax and control that anxiety can also make the person more self-conscious and paradoxically, more anxious.

Imagine that you're a swimmer, standing on the block and preparing to dive into the water. Now, because this is an important ranking tournament, you're rather nervous. As you wait on the block, you realize that your breathing is a bit heightened and your legs are shaking. What do you do? You double down! You try and control this shaking, to get it to stop. When the whistle blows, your feet are so rigidly grounded on the block that it takes you longer to get your feet off the block and dive into the pool. The result is a poor performance, and you chalk this up to you feeling anxious about the race.

Now, what if we were to tell this swimmer not to try and control this shaking? After all, think about a plane that's taking off from a runway. Have you noticed how much the plane shakes just as it's about to lift off? That's when it's gathering the most power, and that is why it's shaking. A better strategy would be to embrace this surge of power and recognize that it's your body energizing itself, preparing to soar.

So next time you're going in for a competition or a big meeting, don't set yourself up for failure. Don't try to go in there 'relaxed'. Instead, accept that you're going to be stressed. Observe these feelings without trying to change them, and accept them as a natural response to the situation. And, if all else fails, remember, everybody else is probably feeling the same way!

Label It Right

We've spoken about the heart pounding, butterflies, and rapid breathing that we experience in anxious situations. But have you ever felt these same feelings in other non-threatening situations? That's right, you've probably experienced them when you're awaiting news of a promotion, going on a first date, or waiting in line for a rollercoaster. These are feelings of arousal—the feeling of being alive, pulsating through your veins. Whether you're feeling afraid or excited, the physical sensations are pretty much alike.

What changes is how we label arousal and subsequently, the meaning we ascribe to it. You can call the same thing fear, and you'll want to run away from it, while when you call it excitement, you'll want to embrace it.

So next time you're about to go on stage to make that speech, let that pounding heart not scare you away—let it remind you that you're ready and excited to take on the new challenge.

Enjoy the Challenge

We automatically think of stress as bad, but have you ever felt stressed and still enjoyed the moment? Perhaps a team project where the entire team was scrambling to meet a deadline? Or a game that went right down to the wire? If you really pause and reflect, you'll find several such moments in your life.

It's never a situation that in itself stresses us out. Instead, it's our perspective of that situation that determines how stressed we feel. This is why two people don't always respond to the same situation in the same way.

When confronted with any situation, we may choose to look at it either from a challenge mindset or a threat mindset. A challenge mindset keeps us in the here and now. We feel excited, look forward to the task, and stay focused on the skills and resources required to manage the situation. In the threat mindset, however, our focus shifts to future 'what ifs', to results, and the risks involved in failure. This mindset automatically puts us on the back foot, and, as we all know, worrying that we might fail actually increases the likelihood of failure.

When caught in a difficult situation, stay in the present moment. Evaluate the resources you have to deal with the problem; relive past successes and rely on your strengths. Trust your training. Hear your heart pound and feel the energy charge through your body. Enjoy the experience of being challenged.

Remember, mountaineers don't ascend Mt Everest

thinking 'what if I fall?' They do it as a challenge to themselves, to get out of their comfort zone, push their limits, and embrace the rush that makes them feel alive!

Creating the Right Resources

How do we develop this challenge mindset? By training for it. As mentioned before, two people don't perceive or respond to a situation in the same way. This is because there's a mediating factor involved known as appraisal. Essentially, when confronted with a demanding situation, our mind first evaluates the resources we have to deal with the situation. If the mind feels that we do have the resources available, then we address the problem head-on, feeling positive and confident. Stress no longer feels like a bad word. On the other hand, if we feel that we don't have the right resources to cope with the pressure, we experience distress, wanting to run away from the situation.

The answer then is practice. We've spoken about it in previous chapters as well; then again, you can never get enough practice. No wonder Sam Snead, the golfer, once said, 'I guess practice puts your brains in your muscles.'

If you want to learn to cope with this pressure, then practise putting yourself in it time and again. Not too much and not consistently, but every now and again, so that you're—in a sense—inoculated against it. Simulate situations that you're going to be confronted with. Remember that the way we perform under pressure is different from how we perform without pressure. It changes our tempo, our decision-making, our muscle tension, and just about everything. Each of these can result in a completely different performance than the ones we've been practising all along.

Thus, practising in isolation isn't enough; you need to practise under pressure. If you want to prepare for an interview, do a mock one. Create all the pressure factors in this interview—the clothes you'll be wearing, the waiting time, the inexplicable expressions of the interviewers, all of it. Besides, of course, preparing you to deal with the pressure, such practice will also give you a sense of self-efficacy. You will go into the meeting knowing that you have prepared for it, and that nothing can throw you off. This confidence alone, in several cases, is enough to see you through.

Podium Finish

1. Stress isn't a bad word. Understand it and harness it.
2. Enjoy the challenge of being tested.
3. Performing under pressure is a skill of its own. Practise it.

Take a moment to think about when you performed your best. How would you describe your energy at that time?

12

Psyching Up! Psyching Down: Strategies for Self-Regulation

'Conscious breathing is a big part, especially in the moments when you're under tension.'

—Novak Djokovic

Noah Lyles was the talk of the town at the 2024 Paris Olympic Games. He won the 100 metres gold medal by five-thousandth of a second! What was even more fascinating than the photo finish was actually his pre-race ritual at the start. Before every race, Noah jumps vertically. People estimate he's able to jump as high as six feet off the ground! As he does, he opens his body wide, and you can see his presence dominate the scene. His arms also open up wide as he makes himself bigger, taking up more space. This is his way of 'psyching up' or energizing himself.

In those two weeks, another champion was emerging, in the swimming pool. Leon Marchand had done what even Michael Phelps hadn't attempted—he won two gold medals in the span of two hours, as the world watched in disbelief. Marchand's demeanour though was completely different from Lyles'. As he stood on the block for his race, there were no big movements. All you could see were deep breaths: breathing in through the nose, out through the mouth.

Regulating Energy

In the previous chapter, we spoke about how stress is inevitable, as is the flight-or-fight response when we experience an adrenaline rush. We also said that trying to 'just relax' isn't going to help, and it'll probably make us even more stressed. That being said, if we take a closer look at the stress–response dynamic, we find that there are opportunities to break this chain and regain control.

All of the changes that our body experiences as a result of stress are caused by the autonomic nervous system. As the name suggests, this part of our nervous system regulates our automatic, involuntary physiological processes—things like heart rate, respiration, blood pressure, digestion, skin temperature, and so on, fall under the control of this autonomic nervous system. Going a step further, there are two parts of this autonomic nervous system: the sympathetic and the parasympathetic nervous systems. The sympathetic nervous system fires up when we're under stress. This is the part of our system involved in the fight–flight response. Once the perception of threat is resolved, the body returns to its normal resting phase. This is done with the help of the actions of the reverse, parasympathetic nervous system.

Let's come back once more to the stress response. We've spoken about quickening heart rate, changing blood pressure, breathing becoming shallower and more rapid, increased metabolism and glucose secretion, sweating, slowing digestion, and so on. Now most of these are things we can't consciously control. There is one though that we can, a process that takes place automatically, but which we can bring under our conscious control, and that is our breathing.

The Mind-Body Feedback Loop

The mind–body feedback loop will come up often when we're talking about performance. It's one of the most powerful mechanisms for bringing about a tangible change. Change any one element, and the entire picture changes. Coming back to the autonomic nervous system, our breathing is the one Trojan horse that we have, which can trick the autonomic nervous system into responding the way that we want it to.

Consider this. If you're fighting a threat, it's only natural that your breathing is going to be quick and shallow. You're not going to have the time to stop for a deep breath. So when do you take that deep breath? When the threat has ended, when you feel safe once more. That 'sigh of relief' is quite literal. It's a signal to our brain that the threat in the environment no longer exists, and so the autonomic nervous system deploys the parasympathetic system to begin the function of repair and rejuvenation. We feel safe and calm, our heart rate reduces, and all the other physiological changes that occur as a result of stress begin to reverse—our body relaxes.

There are two other related changes that also occur when we're stressed. One is where our muscles tighten up, preparing our body to fight. The other is a change in focus, which narrows in on the threat. These two changes, once again, are in our control. Through changing our muscle tension and zone of focus, we can bring about meaningful changes in how our mind and body respond to stressful situations.

We're going to talk about different strategies to energize or relax ourselves. Before that, let's take a minute to understand what that ideal level of energy is. After all, in the last chapter we spoke about how stress is an energizer. Now we're talking about how to reduce that stress. What's the final verdict on stress? Is it good or bad? Should it be avoided or embraced? How much is too much?

Find Your Zone

More than a hundred years back, psychologists formulated a relationship between arousal and performance known as the Yerkes-Dodson law. It is represented in the shape of an inverted U. It states that performance increases with arousal, up to a certain point. Without any arousal, there is no real stimulus, and no motivation for us to do anything. On the other hand, if the arousal increases beyond a point, it overwhelms us and negatively impacts our performance.

More recent research suggests a variation of this law, referring to the concept as the 'individual zone of optimal functioning' or IZOF. According to the IZOF, as the name suggests, each person has their own optimal arousal at which they perform their best. Just how individualized these zones are is apparent when you watch how Lyles and Marchand compete.

Psyching Down

The right amount of arousal depends on two key factors: one is the nature of the activity, and the other is your own zone of what works well for you. Our mental or psychological state is in our control. With the right techniques, we have the ability to increase or decrease the psychological intensity or arousal we experience in any given situation, thereby allowing us to perform optimally. We use the term 'psyching down' when talking about strategies that reduce our body's stress levels.

As mentioned before, breathing is probably the most effective tool in your hands. Deep breathing, in a way that consciously involves the diaphragm, is most effective. When breathing deep, give more importance to your exhalation. While breathing in is associated with heart rate acceleration, exhalation is associated with heart rate deceleration. So make sure that your exhalation is at least as long as, if not longer than, the time you take to inhale. A quick and powerful exhale through the mouth is also effective—it's something you'll find athletes doing quite often in the moments right before they begin their performance. This leads to a sharp deceleration in your heart rate, which can have a facilitative impact on your performance.

Entire books can be written about the various aspects of breathwork. Though they are beyond the scope of this particular book, it may be worthwhile for you to delve deeper into this science.

There are other strategies beyond breathwork which involve muscle relaxation. Body scans and progressive muscle relaxation, where you systematically clench and then relax various muscles in the body, can also help reduce the physical tension you feel.

Also, keep in mind to stay away from substances that can increase your arousal—caffeine being one of the greatest culprits. We often tend to rely on caffeine, especially when we're racing against a deadline or anxiously preparing for an exam. Players often have a cup of coffee on the morning of their competition. Keep in mind though that if you're stressed about a deadline or competition, your arousal is already heightened. Caffeine is only going to increase your arousal further, tipping you over to the other side of the curve.

To psych down, we need to create a relaxed environment, both internally and externally. Visualizing calming imagery like a beach or a mountain can replace anxious thoughts and take your mind into a relaxed state. Soft, relaxing music can also have a similar impact, allowing our body to gradually sync with the rhythm of the tune. Speaking slowly in a soft tone and low pitch can all have similar effects as well.

These psyching-down strategies are particularly useful when we need our body to be more relaxed. We earlier spoke about shooting, where athletes train to shoot between two heartbeats. It may also help while performing other precision tasks, like a surgery that requires our hands to be steady.

Psyching up

Every performance task that we take up doesn't need us to be calm and composed all the time. Our performance in certain tasks does improve when we're pumped up. So this high-energy fight–flight response can actually be quite effective in activities requiring explosive energy. It can help in races, combat sport or any other sport that involves brute force and strength. It can also help energize us during a public speaking event, a high-stakes negotiation or a dance performance.

Just like we can trick our autonomic nervous system into feeling calmer, we can employ the reverse strategies to psych up higher. So replace the deep breaths with quick, shallow breathing. Use quick movements, hops and jumps. Listen to fast-paced music with beats that make you feel more energized. Use power imagery instead of relaxing ones—perhaps an animal preparing to pounce! These strategies can also help absorb our already anxious energy and transform it into something that feels more energetic and exciting.

A Common Mistake

When choking under pressure, we often forget these basics like breathing. Even at times when we try to breathe consciously, and try to relax ourselves, nothing works. We end up feeling more anxious, and subsequently more helpless.

The most common mistake we make in such a situation is attempting such strategies directly during performance or in competition situations. For peak performance, we have to think of our mind and body as tools to be chiselled over time with conscious, consistent effort.

If you find yourself unable to regulate your energy during such times, start training yourself to self-regulate in practice situations. Practice works on the principles of conditioning, which is one of the primary ways in which human beings learn anything new. Initially, attempt breathing exercises in a state when you're already calm and relaxed, rather than in situations where you're on edge. It's the same with visualizations and muscle relaxation as well. It's so that your body is more accustomed to these feelings of relaxation. The idea is to train them so well that when your muscles tighten, your mind remembers and automatically relaxes them, without you having to make a very deliberate effort. Practising breathwork regularly allows us to enter into this state of relaxation a lot quicker.

At the end of the day, don't fear stress. It's not something new, unusual, or something we can't deal with. All that it is is a surge of energy. What you need to do is to train yourself with the knowledge, skill and practice to regulate and eventually harness that energy.

Podium Finish

1. You can regulate your energy.
2. Reflect on your past wins. Identify the zone in which you perform your best.
3. Find that one technique that can energize or relax you.

Do you tend to feel anxious in the hours and days leading up to a big event?

13

Playing the Waiting Game: Getting into the Zone

'I put the two bottles down at my feet... It's a way of placing myself in a match, ordering my surroundings to match the order I seek in my head.'

–Rafael Nadal

Before every serve, Rafael Nadal adjusts his shorts and then both sleeves of his shirt. He then puts his hair behind his ears and wipes his nose as he bounces the ball. After a few more bounces, he serves the ball. It's been over two decades watching Nadal play, and this routine has been consistent through pretty much every single point he's ever played.

This right here is a pre-point routine. It's nowhere near as evident as in Nadal's serve, but if you look closely, you'll find most elite athletes with their own version of a pre-performance routine.

The Waiting Game

Have you noticed when it is that you feel the most anxious in any performance situation? Look closely and you'll realize that it's usually not when you're actually performing, but rather, it's in the time when you're waiting idle, right before the performance. Remember how you feel sitting in the exam hall, waiting for your question paper, dreading what's coming your way?

This is also why tennis is known to be one of the most mentally challenging games. Yes, the physicality and duration of the game can test any player. But beyond that, it's also a game of waiting. Watching a game of tennis, you may not realize the amount of downtime that's involved in the sport. In fact, about 10 years back, *The Wall Street Journal* timed the action in a match that lasted two hours and 41 minutes. You'll be surprised to learn that the actual play time was only about 26 minutes. Imagine the amount of time players have in between points, and the sheer volume of thoughts that find their way in.

Anxiety is usually not a response to a threat in the present, but rather to a situation in the future. We call this 'anticipatory anxiety'. It's when your mind is throwing up every worst-case scenario, the adrenaline is rushing through your system, and yet, there's nothing you can do but wait and watch. In that moment, there's no way to turn that nervous energy into action. For some players, this kind of anticipatory anxiety is so telling that they perform better when their match is in the morning hours, as compared to playing in the evening. There's just so much more time to dwell. For many of us, this anticipatory anxiety can begin up to several days before an important event. That's also what explains the sleepless nights.

Don't Think Twice

This anticipatory anxiety is all about our thoughts. Thoughts, in fact, are often the most significant distractions to peak performance. Yet, we also need our thoughts to guide us to take the right actions. One way to understand this dichotomy is to use Kahneman's systems of thinking.

Nobel Prize winner Daniel Kahneman, in his book *Thinking Fast and Slow*, highlighted two systems of thinking: System 1 is fast, intuitive and effortless; System 2 is slow, conscious, analytical and deliberate. Each of these systems has a place in our everyday decision-making. Preparation requires a lot more of system 2—more effortful and deliberate. Once the hours of practice add up, response patterns develop and these actions become more automatic and intuitive. When executing a skill, moments of peak performance come from system 1 firing—what people have often described as a feeling of flow. An everyday example of this is riding a cycle. Once you've learnt how to cycle, you can easily ride the cycle at 20 kmph, in a straight line, without giving it a second thought. But now imagine if we ask you to ride the cycle slowly and carefully, sticking to a straight line drawn on the ground. Suddenly, a process that was automatic becomes deliberate. Chances are, you're going to find it a lot more difficult to ride the cycle in that straight line now. The chances of you falling are also going to drastically increase.

This rule applies to all skills. Learning the skill requires slow, deliberate practice. Executing it, on the other hand, requires you to be intuitive and effortless. Hence, you may have heard many elite athletes talk about feeling 'blank' just before starting a competition.

Pre-Performance Routines

The mind at this time isn't actually 'blank'. Instead, it's so focused on the present moment, on the here and now, that unwanted thoughts have no place. The way athletes achieve this is through pre-performance routines.

Coming back to tennis, think about why a tennis player bounces a ball so many times before actually serving. It's not like bouncing the ball is going to add some extra force that'll make the serve faster. This is a pre-performance routine, a technique players use to zone in. It's simple behaviour, nothing too complex. It allows the player to focus on the feel of the ball as they grasp it, watch its movement and hear a rhythm. As the player focuses on these external stimuli, their mind no longer has space to think unnecessary thoughts. In fact, in this way, our thoughts and our behaviours have an inverse relationship. The more actively we engage with our environment, the less we think. The more disengaged we are, allowing ourselves to sit in one place and stare into space, the more unnecessary thoughts are going to flood in.

Pre-performance routines break the chain of unhelpful thoughts and worries and take us away from our self-consciousness. With simple behavioural movements, they gently take us into a flow state, which then activates the body's muscle memory. Without giving it much of a thought then, the player looks at the point where they want to serve, throws up the ball, and the body executes the serve effortlessly. These pre-performance routines aren't restricted to a particular sport or even to sport at all. They can be used in any situation involving skill execution.

Virender Sehwag had an interesting take on pre-performance routines. When facing a ball coming at you at close to 160 kmph, you'd think you want to be focused and stare intently at the ball. But no, at that moment, you'll find Sehwag singing a song: 'Chala jaata hoon…kisi ki dhun mein…' is one of his favourites. In fact, he was so famous for his singing that players standing nearby, like wicketkeepers and slip fielders from other teams, used to sometimes request songs!

When a ball is coming at that pace, you can't consciously think about how you should play the ball. You have to rely on your instincts (which you would have honed by stacking repetitions during training). Sehwag was known for his quick reflexes and hand-eye coordination. Singing these songs then helped to keep his thoughts away. Instead, they kept him focused on the ball and ensured that he played one shot at a time, to the merit of the ball.

The Long Haul

What we've spoken about so far is the use of pre-performance routines in the minutes, or even seconds, leading up to skill performance. But like we mentioned before, the stress and overthinking related to an important event can sometimes start several hours or even days before.

On match day, the mental preparation doesn't start when the player enters the arena. It starts when they wake up. Players will often eat the same breakfast they eat before all their competitions. They pack their bags a certain way, and perhaps practise some mindfulness and visualization training on the day. Each player has a preferred playlist of songs or at least the kind of music that they listen to in the hours before the game. They may talk to friends or family, read a book, watch an inspiring clip, or pray. Their training drills and warm-ups will also be consistent on match days. The fact that players follow these routines each and every time makes them automatic, minimizing mental effort, but keeps the person engaged in a flow of activities. It allows them to spend their time actively engaged, keeping that anticipatory anxiety away. It's not that they don't rest, but even that rest is active. From the moment they wake up, till it's show time, the mind is on a leash. These pre-performance routines don't allow the mind the opportunity to wander here and there. They keep our minds still and our actions purposeful.

Find Your Routine

You'll seldom find two players with an identical pre-game routine. That's because different things work for different people. Don't copy someone else's routine as is. Observe and learn from people; but, at the end of the day, focus on what works for you. And, of course, we can't say this enough, PRACTISE! Not just in performance situations, but in training as well. Without practice, these are simply a set of disconnected actions. With practice, they're your pre-game routine that can get you into the zone.

Podium Finish

1. Anticipatory anxiety is one of the greatest culprits of performance pressure.
2. Master the waiting game by creating your own pre-performance routine.
3. Stay engaged, stay focused, stay relaxed.

Do you regret taking an
action on impulse?

14

Taming Instinct: From Reacting to Responding

'The first thing is to be patient, which is probably the hardest thing to do.'

—Shane Warne

The England football team hasn't always seen the best of times with penalty shootouts. Prior to the World Cup in 2018, they hadn't won a match on penalty shootouts since 1996. Whether it was Steven Gerrard, David Beckham, Frank Lampard or Ashley Cole, they had all missed.

Back in 1996, it was Gareth Southgate, the youngest and least-capped member of the starting line-up. Before that fateful evening, his club record read one taken, one missed. It was the semi-final of the Euro '96 against Germany. Minutes before the penalty shootout went underway, Southgate was asked if he'd be the sixth man, if it went down to the wire. He agreed. In his own words, the walk to the penalty spot took forever, the entire world's eyes on him. He was unprepared and anxious. In this battle of wits, as he walked down, with a goalkeeper a mere 12 yards away, Southgate hit a 'soft and badly placed penalty'. In the blink of an eye, England saw their championship dreams go up in smoke once more.

Penalty shootouts have a bad rep. Teams like England have dismissed them as sheer luck, akin to winning a lottery. Southgate, however, who had over two decades to think about that moment, felt otherwise. It wasn't like flipping a coin. After all, even a coin flip has a 50–50 chance. England has had unfavourable results 86 per cent of the time. No, there is more to a penalty shootout than luck. It is about performing a skill under pressure, and a battle of nerves; it is about shouldering responsibility for the entire team, and the expectations of millions of spectators.

Experiential Avoidance

In his autobiography, Southgate described that moment: 'All I wanted was the ball: put it over and done with.' It's not unusual, this thought. When we experience a sense of discomfort, all we want is for that moment to be over. Have you ever noticed yourself doing things faster when you're anxious? It happens quite frequently during public speaking. When we feel a negative emotion, we naturally give in to the immediate need to feel better. In fact, in a way, it's similar to what goes on even when we're angry. When the distress is too much to handle, we tend to behave in ways to rid ourselves of the feeling quickly. The aim becomes to get instant relief—we lash out. Sometimes people even end up quitting their jobs in the heat of the moment. There's an odd sense of relief that quitting brings. Only problem is, it doesn't last long. We act on impulse, even if that means harming ourselves in the long run.

In a Split Second

After 20 years, Gareth Southgate found himself at the helm of the England football team. As manager of the Three Lions, Southgate was determined not to let history repeat itself. With all the technology and sport science expertise in his arsenal, he set out to determine the factors that led England to perform so poorly at penalty shootouts. The answer lay in the fraction of a second. Analysts discovered that English players had the quickest reaction time of all national teams. This reaction time refers to the time from when the referee blows the whistle to the moment at which the player starts his run up to the ball. This was found to be 0.28 seconds. There was a sense of rush. The run-up to the ball wasn't out of their own initiative. Rather, it was a kneejerk reaction to the sound of the whistle; an attempt to get the shot over and done with.

Take Responsibility

We believe our impulsive responses to be out of our control. Whether it's bouts of aggression or choking under pressure, we often look at these with a sense of helplessness. 'It's just the way I am.' 'I just can't help myself.' 'It's just my bad luck.' The biggest problem with England's approach to the penalty, prior to 2018, was their tendency to believe that it was all about luck, and that there was nothing they could do about it. In fact, many teams also don't give sufficient emphasis to penalties in shootouts, believing that it's impossible to recreate the same environment and the same pressure that is integral to the lived experience of a real penalty kick. So why bother? The first step is then to take the onus of one's emotional responses. They are our emotions, they are of our own making, and it's *on us* to learn how best to control them.

It's true that our impulses can catch us off guard, making us feel that we are at their mercy. The key really is to anticipate the triggers that make us react in unhelpful ways and reprogramme our responses to them. Just like the England team did a data analysis, notice the patterns you follow. What are the situations that make you anxious, what are the triggers that make you angry? And, more importantly, introspect on how it is that you actually respond when confronted with these situations.

Pause

Ever noticed that after making one mistake, the odds of making another mistake actually increase? It's similar to when players lose five to six points in a streak, each mistake building on to the previous one and affecting our confidence, our decision making, and our performance as a whole. It's a negative psychological momentum of sorts. What we need to do is break the cycle and regain perspective.

When things seem like they're going out of control, slow down. Take a break. Just pause for a moment. Athletes do this quite often. Small hacks like taking a moment longer to serve, towelling before the next point, or, in some cases, even bending down to tie one's shoelaces—these are all techniques used by players to slow the tempo.

Our actions often occur in a series of simple stimulus-response associations. We receive a stimulus and our mind, which is conditioned to respond in a certain way, carries out the reaction in an unthinking manner. Hear the whistle, run to the ball—it doesn't have to be that way.

So if you find yourself getting angry or feeling nervous, just pause. Take a deep breath and re-evaluate the path your momentum is taking you down. Ask yourself, is that really where you want to be going? Probably not. So, make a choice in that moment. Take back control; acknowledge your feelings but don't let them get in the driver's seat.

Ground Yourself in the Present

When emotions take over, our thoughts go into a spiral. All our past failures and future apprehensions come hurtling at us. We get so wrapped up in our thoughts that we lose sight of the present moment. In the little while when you take that pause, ground yourself in the present. Feel the texture of the towel brush your face, hear the sounds that surround you, feel your feet on the ground, and breathe in the air that fills your lungs. Activate your senses and pay attention to the sights, sounds, smells, colours and touch surrounding you.

Retrain Your Instincts

Just as with all other aspects of mental training, controlling reactions doesn't come to us immediately. It's something we need to anticipate and plan for. In the case of England in 2018, they made a script of what the penalty shootout would look like. They didn't leave much to chance. They decided the order in which the players would take the shots, so they no longer felt compelled to 'volunteer'. They recreated the 'tired legs' and the pressure within practice situations, so the players were prepared for what it would feel like to play through the fatigue. Rather than the players gathering the ball, they got the goalkeeper to personally hand over the ball to the next striker, to keep the environment even more under their control. Players were taught to pause and hit the shot not when the whistle blew, but when they were ready, on their own terms. They were encouraged to hit the shot to their natural side rather than second-guessing themselves.

If you've identified a situation where the odds of your anxiety taking over are higher, make a plan for that situation. Make a game plan, and minimize the uncontrollable factors. Become aware of the mistakes you're likely to make and actively work towards training your mind to create a new default.

Viktor Frankl, a psychiatrist, existentialist and Holocaust survivor, once quoted, 'Between stimulus and response there is a space. In that space is our power to choose our response. In our response lies our freedom.' Frankl never specified how big that space was, but sometimes even a split second can be enough.

Podium Finish

1. Don't avoid discomfort.
2. Don't be guided by impulses. Learn to pause.
3. Practise your responses to develop a new kind of instinct.

Take a look in the mirror. What does your body language communicate to the world?

15

To Di World: Lessons in Body Language

'I'm not going to tell you I'm going to be the best. I'm going to show you.'

—Usain Bolt

If you want to understand the power of body language, watch the New Zealand All Blacks perform the customary Haka before their rugby matches. The entire team gathers to participate in a traditional Māori war dance. Imagine the entire team, dressed in all black, knees bent, leaning forward, tongues sticking out, fiery eyes staring at their opponents, thumping their chests, and chanting in unison. It's a sight to behold. You don't need to understand the words to feel the goosebumps.

Besides honouring their cultural roots, the Haka is a ritual that brings the team together and energizes them. It's a show of brute force, strength and unity. Imagine the impact on the opponents!

Body 'Language'

Think of an image of a confident person. You'll imagine the person standing tall and steady, back straight, and shoulders relaxed. You'll imagine them looking straight ahead and making eye contact, probably even smiling. On the other hand, if you're to think of a person who's nervous or underconfident, you'll imagine someone making themselves smaller, almost crouching a bit—back hunched, shoulders rolled inwards, looking down or away. You may also notice some jitteriness in their hands and legs. Without saying a single word, so much is being communicated!

It's called a language because that's exactly what it is. Our body is probably one of the most important tools of communication. In this manner, it's not possible to not communicate. If we're in the presence of another, we are communicating *something*. The idea is to then make sure that this communication is effective and leads to the results that we want.

Staring down an opponent is one way to intimidate them. Appearing relaxed, unfazed, sometimes even smiling at the aggression of another is yet another way. A look of frustration or helplessness can boost the confidence of your opponent and reduce trust in a key stakeholder.

First Impressions

Did you know that it sometimes takes less than a tenth of a second for someone to form a first impression about you? Other cognitive biases then swoop in and ensure that these first impressions stick. And no matter how accurate or faulty—or the subsequent information learnt about the individual—this impression can have a significant impact on several aspects of life, including our career and relationships. Body language is perhaps one of the most important elements that impacts these first impressions, and that, amongst many other reasons, is what makes them so powerful.

The Language of Confidence

Here are some essentials when it comes to portraying confidence in your body language. Keep your back straight, take a deep breath, and allow your chest to expand and fill up with confidence. Relax your shoulders and your facial muscles. Keep an open stance, that is, don't cross your arms—it'll portray being closed off or disinterested. Stand firm and tall, distributing your weight equally to both your legs. Practise a firm handshake. Avoid fidgeting or shifting your gaze; maintain eye contact with whoever you meet and, most importantly, don't forget to smile!

Suit up!

It's not just our actions and postures that impact perceptions; it's also how we groom ourselves and the clothes we wear. It may be hard to believe, but several studies have found that players and teams that wear the colour red—a colour associated with aggression and dominance—actually win more! It's also why people choose to wear a red tie at certain occasions that demand a show of strength and authority. While the colour of a jersey or tie alone can never be the determining factor for success, it certainly does leave an impression! So next time you're going in for an interview, an important presentation, or just any situation where you want to create an impact, take a moment to think about how the clothes you wear make you feel about yourself, and how you want to present yourself to others.

The Mind-Body Feedback Loop

Body language isn't just about communicating with others, you can also think of it as another kind of self-talk. Simply put, while we're all aware that our mood impacts our body language, our body language can also impact our mood!

A study conducted in 1988 found that participants who read a cartoon or article while holding a pencil horizontally between their teeth actually found the article funnier. This was because such a task 'forced' the person's face into the shape of a smile, thus sending a message to the brain that the person was happy. (Go ahead and try it yourself! See if putting a finger horizontally in between your teeth brings about any changes in your mood!)

You'll also notice this feedback loop in your everyday life. If you're tense, it's likely that your shoulders are raised close to your ears, or your face is frozen in a frown. Just making a conscious effort to relax your shoulders and eyebrows at this time can change the way you feel. It's a similar thing with confidence. If you're feeling underconfident and find yourself slouching, just take a deep breath and straighten your back. A simple action like this will actually trick your mind into feeling more confident.

Train Your Body Language

In an interview with P.V. Sindhu and her coach Pullela Gopichand, after her 2016 Rio Olympics medal, the duo spoke about how Gopichand had encouraged Sindhu to scream during her matches. It's not something that came naturally to her at all! In fact, they spoke of a time when Sindhu had to stand in the centre and everyone else at the academy was asked to stop playing until she could muster the courage to shout. It was an important skill for her to learn, for her to portray this raw force out there on the court.

Just like every other element of performance, don't expect the right body language to just come to you automatically. It's something we need to make part of our performance routine, something we need to train. When practising, be aware of your body language and what you're communicating. Practising your body language in front of a mirror, or getting feedback on it from a trusted other, can help. When you visualize your performance, keep an eye on the kind of body language you're displaying.

If you've been doing it for years, your body may keep returning to its default patterns of slouching or becoming smaller in other ways. Become aware of this tendency and work towards intentionally changing it in your everyday interactions. Before stepping out there, remind yourself to take up a confident posture. Make it a part of your pre-performance routine. After every break, as you resume your work, take a moment to adopt a confident, relaxed stance.

Choose Confidence

There's a term known as 'illusion of transparency', which is a phenomenon that often contributes to social anxiety. We have a tendency to believe that everyone around us knows exactly how we're feeling and what's going on in our minds. That people can somehow make out just how nervous or down we are in that moment. This, like many others, is a cognitive bias. It's not really true. People can't see through us, they can't tell how anxious or nervous we are just by looking at us. What they see is what we choose to show—the instrumental word being *choose*. No matter the internal state, no matter the fears or self-doubt, you can choose to portray confidence, and with that choice, you also make the choice to embrace that confidence. All you need to do is learn the language.

Podium Finish

1. Body language shapes perceptions.
2. The mind and body communicate with one another.
3. Take control of what you're communicating to the world, and to yourself.

Do you think luck plays
a role in success?

16

Charms and Chances: Creating Your Own Luck

'I just did a little wink in the camera and everybody loved it! It gives me good luck. I win a lot of races with my luck.'

—Shaolin Sandor Liu

Think back to the last exam you took. Any chance you were carrying your favourite 'lucky' pen or ruler? Do you have a lucky charm, something you rely on for important moments in your life? It could be a lucky tie, a pair of shoes, a locket you wear, a gesture you carry out, or even a person you speak to each time before you set forth.

For many of us, good-luck charms have a mystical appeal. Others may scoff at these 'silly superstitions'. Yet, it's something that many of us have resorted to at some point in our lives. In fact, studies believe that we tend to engage in such behaviours when we experience feelings of uncertainty, when we're very stressed out, and, most of all, when we don't feel much in control of the situation. Sounds familiar?

Given these conditions, it's seen that such beliefs are most prevalent amongst students and sportspeople, but the same can also be seen amongst people who are exposed to any form of performance tasks—a high-risk procedure, an interview, a marquee event, or even a date.

A Short History of Shorts

Ever wondered why basketball shorts are as baggy as they are? We've often asked people this question, and the response we've gotten almost every time is, so that players can move faster and jump higher. That's a bit unfair when you think about all the other sports that may require the same amount of speed and agility, right? The real reason actually has been traced back to a trend inadvertently started by the one and only Michael Jordan. Now we've all heard of MJ, famous for his prolific leaps and slam dunks, which earned him the title 'His Airness'. But before signing with the Chicago Bulls, Jordan used to play for the North Carolina Tar Heels, his varsity team. Legend has it that even as he moved on to the NBA, there's one thing he couldn't let go of from his university days—his North Carolina basketball shorts. And it's not just that he carried them around with him when he went for tournaments; he used to wear them under his Chicago Bulls shorts, which is why he decided to make those a few sizes larger. A trend soon followed with other basketballers opting for larger shorts, and today, that's become the new normal.

Michael Jordan isn't the only athlete who believes in lucky charms. Sachin Tendulkar always wore his left pad first. He even played with his same lucky but rather battered bat, even if that meant taping it up for an important game. Bjorn Borg grew a 'lucky beard' in time for the first round of Wimbledon every year. What's most amusing is that these 'odd' behaviours aren't restricted to the players themselves, even the spectators join in—our personal favourite being one where ardent fans sit absolutely still and refuse to move from their chairs, for hours on end, fearing that any move of theirs might cost their team the match. If we're being completely honest, we've done it ourselves too.

The Science behind Lucky Charms

That so many leading sporting personalities in the world depend on these lucky charms sounds counter-intuitive at first. Shouldn't a successful person rather depend on their own skills and abilities than on something so insignificant and unrelated to the task at hand? To study the effect of good-luck charms on performance, a team of psychologists recruited participants for a golf-putting challenge, where they were required to get 10 putts from a distance of 100 cm. To some participants, the researchers said, 'This is the ball everyone has used so far'; to others they said, 'Here is your ball. So far, it's turned out to be a lucky ball.' Results showed that the participants who had been told about the lucky ball scored better in the challenge than those who hadn't been told the same.

The Power of Belief

So, was it the ball which was lucky? Probably not. Instead, it was the participants' *belief* in the luck that impacted their performance, a kind of psychological placebo. The more people believe in good luck, the more optimistic and confident they tend to be. It also increases our sense of self-efficacy. In previous chapters, we've spoken about the role of self-efficacy, and how belief in one's own capability to succeed in a particular situation improves their performance. The reason behind this is manyfold. The less the self-doubt, the more we're able to trust our performance. No longer plagued by overthinking, it's easier to get into a flow state. At the same time, people who believe that they can achieve a task also set more challenging goals for themselves and, more importantly, don't give up as easily. Without a doubt, it is the ability to persevere in the face of uncertainty that is the cornerstone of success.

A Positive Illusion of Control

We don't lead our lives in a silo. Many external factors impact our day-to-day life. The fact of the matter is, we often find ourselves in situations where despite our best efforts, things aren't 100 per cent in our control. The element of chance is ever-present, and this unpredictability of life can sometimes be a real dampener to motivation. When confronted with uncertain outcomes, you might hear yourself saying 'what's the point of trying anyway'. It's in these cases where we need to believe that we have control over the situation, and do everything in our power to strengthen this belief. To do this, we plan, we train, we anticipate. But along with all of this hard work, a little faith in good luck doesn't hurt. In moments when we feel our resolve shake, it's this faith that can provide the strength and solace we need. Knowing that you have luck on your side, you feel more positive, more in control of the situation, and thereby more committed to giving it everything you've got!

A Calming Influence

Performance and competition have the power to make us nervous. As we enter important performance situations, it's common to experience feelings of restlessness, agitation, trembling, palpitation, and so on. Thoughts of failure and self-doubt begin to create havoc in our mind. Because we associate rituals and lucky charms with past successes, and because these objects or actions offer us a sense of emotional comfort and dependence, engaging in these behaviours can actually have a soothing effect on us. They can shift our thoughts from past failures to successes, and transform self-doubt into self-resolve, all the while calming down our nervous bodily responses. While these rituals and charms in themselves may be entirely unrelated to the outcome of the match, they still do have an outcome, that is, how we *feel* before and during the game, and subsequently how we perform.

Finding 'Your' Mojo: A Word of Caution

Effort and hard work are precursors to success, and there are no substitutes. Finding the means to create positive associations and trigger self-affirming beliefs, however, can be a useful addition. These don't have to be fixed objects, rituals or processes that work; they can be entirely idiosyncratic. To find your lucky charm, if you don't already have one, dig deep into your memories and look for moments where you felt confident and were successful. If you're someone who already believes in good luck, follow those behaviours unabashedly. You now have the studies to back you up.

Just a word of caution before we end this chapter: Lucky charms work very well in situations that have an element of chance but also require skill. However, don't rely on them for high-risk activities that have a huge potential for losses. It's good to be a little less optimistic and a little more cautious in such endeavours.

Podium Finish

1. Luck isn't a substitute for skill or effort.
2. Create your own personal rituals and charms for success.
3. Rituals foster belief and confidence. Use them well.

Have you ever felt like things
were spiralling out of control?

17

Time Out: Breaks for Peak Performance

'It is amazing how many drivers, even at the Formula One Level, think that the brakes are for slowing the car down.'

—Mario Andretti

We believe that to be successful, we have to be relentless. That letting up for even a moment can result in someone else taking the lead. For a star performer, the idea of taking a break can be quite daunting.

To understand the true value of breaks, let's turn for a moment to Formula One racing. These cars race at an average speed of about 200 mph. It's safe to say, you have to be fast if you want to compete. Yet, an F1 champion is not someone who only knows how to rev up the engines and drive the car at full throttle. More importantly, it's someone who knows when to slow down, when to pull the brakes, and when to make those much-needed pit stops. Taking breaks at the right time really is, at the end of the day, about staying in control.

Catch a Breather

Breaks are important for recovery. And here we're not just talking about physical recovery, we're talking about mental recovery too. Taking a break is not just about lying down or sitting on a couch, staring into space, or scrolling one reel after another. These kinds of breaks can actually be quite counterproductive. The reason is that while such breaks rest our body, they keep our mind overstimulated. When the mind is not focused on one thing, it tends to wander. The overthinking results in us feeling even more mentally exhausted than before. It's similar with too much screen time as well. If you are studying or doing a desk job, then reading or scrolling during a break isn't going to help. In times like these, you need to activate your body and calm your mind. The idea is to switch it up and give your mind and body a break from what they were previously doing.

Regroup

Certain situations have the capacity to throw us off our game. Such as an unexpected blow that jolts us, disorients us, and leaves us vulnerable. Think of it like a well-timed punch that strikes you square in the face. Coupled with the disorientation, even though you're not altogether focused, you may feel the urge to fight back harder or shut down and withdraw. What's best in such situations is actually to do neither and take a break instead. This doesn't have to be a very long break—just anything that can stop the negative spiral and reduce the odds of an impulsive action. In a boxing ring, this can be taking a step back, shifting the focus to your breathing and coming back in. During an exam, it can be putting the pen down and taking a sip of water. In a fit of anger, it can be leaving the room for a minute to calm down. In each of these, a slight shift can break the pattern and help regain control over one's physical and emotional reactions.

Planned Breaks

Do you know how long it takes to replace the tyres of a car during an F1 pit stop? Under two seconds. McLaren, in fact, completed a pit stop in 1.8 seconds. A team of 20 people coming together to replace all four wheels and making quick adjustments, all in 1.8 seconds—how do they do this? It's possible with meticulous planning and preparation. Yes, even breaks have to be planned if we want to really optimize their effects. So, if you've recognized what your potential pitfalls may be, or situations where you may struggle, prepare in advance. Know what works for you, and practise it.

Make sure that it's an intentional break, a kind of active rest. Even in your breaks, either your hands or your mind should be focused on doing a simple task. A break that involves any kind of deliberate physical action keeps us in the present moment, prevents overthinking, and allows us to bounce back faster.

Resetting Rhythms

One of the most palpable responses to stress that we experience is a change in our rhythm. Notice how when you're stressed you may start talking too fast or the pitch of your voice may change. You may eat fast, react impulsively, or interrupt another. All of these are signs that our mind and body are getting agitated. The opposite is also true of the stress response, where we slow down more than usual. In trying to control this agitation, we resort to overthinking, over-planning, and over-preparing. All of these are disruptions to our rhythm—our mind and body keep racing at different speeds, and we cannot quite keep performing the way that we should be.

Taking a break in such a case is invaluable. Trying to recalibrate this rhythm without taking a break can lead us to overcompensating. A refresh is a much better option. A time out at such a moment not only breaks the poor rhythm, but also gives us an opportunity to look back and reflect—what are we thinking? What are we feeling? What are the thoughts and emotions we're responding to? Giving ourselves even this fleeting opportunity to reconnect with ourselves is often enough to get back in the groove.

Just like you can pull the brakes on your own negative reactions, you can also break the rhythm of an opponent who's riding high on momentum. The sense of flow that one achieves during a performance has a lot to do with tempo and timing, and any kind of disruption to that tempo can actually disrupt that state of flow. So, if you find yourself struggling against an opponent, or making one mistake after another, take a break. This can be a strategic timeout or just delaying getting back into the game. Nothing too drastic, even a few seconds here is enough. Something as simple as keeping your racket down to tie a shoelace can be enough to break this rhythm—your own as well as your opponent's. The dynamics are similar across situations. This same strategy isn't restricted to a badminton or tennis court, it can work just as well in a court of law, or perhaps a conference room.

Switch off–Switch back on

Ever had a mobile phone or laptop that glitched? Your go-to response will be to restart it, and voila! In all likelihood, it will start to work smoothly once more. What happened here? The restart cleared out the RAM and the phone started working once more, without those random bits of memory slowing down its functioning.

Lucky for us, the mind works the same way in some sense. Have you noticed that when something untoward happens, we keep thinking about it, perhaps even reliving it for several minutes, days or weeks after it? This is where the switch on–switch off technique comes into play.

It's easy to see how this technique plays out in cricket, though the same can be extrapolated across sport and life situations. Ben Stokes is one such cricketer who is known to have used this strategy. In an interview, he said, 'Switching on when it matters and switching off when you can is key to managing the mental demands of cricket. It helps me stay focused during the important moments and relaxed during breaks.' Looking around, taking off the glove, or walking to speak to a partner can be ways of switching off, whereas putting the glove back on, taking guard and focusing once more on the bowler can be ways to switch back on.

To use this technique, think of the attentional demands that are placed when you need to do the task you've set out to do. Evaluate it really closely. Don't think of a game of golf as a five-hour game; think of it as 72 shots. Between every two shots is a break, and each shot is independent of the one before and after it. A play is not a two-hour performance, it's a series of independent scenes strung together.

There are two benefits to approaching tasks this way. First, it helps avoid the domino effect if things go wrong. Not knowing one answer need not affect how we approach the next question. Second, it helps us conserve our finite focus resource. By giving ourselves a break in our focus, we can approach every new opportunity with the same laser focus.

Now, we know that we mentioned earlier that focus can't really be switched off, and that's true. When we talk about switching off, we simply mean relaxing our focus and shifting it to something that's not task-related. So between two questions, take a quick micro-break. Take a deep breath, maybe stretch your back. For a slightly longer break, have a sip of water, or look outside the window. For this strategy to work, focus on the water, on the trees outside, not on the questions or how others around you are doing. And after a couple of moments, bring your focus back to your question paper, and get cracking on the next question.

Breaks as Motivators

An additional benefit of taking breaks is that it automatically splits a large daunting task into smaller bite-sized elements. Several researchers have spoken about the benefits of techniques such as the Pomodoro, where people grappling with procrastination are encouraged to break down large tasks into 25-minute work sprints, followed by short five-minute breaks. This way, breaks can help us take things one step at a time, rather than getting overwhelmed by everything we have to do. Doing something enjoyable in that break can also give us something to look forward to, which can serve as a reward for finishing the task we've set ourselves in that short sprint. It's also a great way of staying accountable—we don't need to wait till the very end of the day to look back. Every few minutes can be an opportunity to reflect and course-correct.

Time It Right

When we're in the flow, we don't usually like to take breaks. Instead, we think about breaks when we're depleted, or stuck at a certain point. That means that we've left whatever we're doing at a stage to where it's unpleasant to return. With this negative association in mind, it's not that odd then that we find it difficult to return to the task at hand, choosing instead to procrastinate further. A better idea is to actually take a break *before* we exhaust ourselves. This way, we take a break, still wanting to do more. We also end up enjoying our breaks a lot more because we still have energy reserves to do the things that we enjoy. And because we look forward to doing things that we are good at, we're excited to get back to the work we're doing, because we know the next steps and look forward to giving it a go.

Tips to Take an Effective Break

Reading about how to take a break might sound a bit odd, after all, it's what should come to all of us most intuitively. We all take breaks all the time. But the way we take a break can actually have a significant impact on how positively or negatively it affects us.

Yes, it is possible for a break to affect us negatively. How can this happen? We often take breaks that tire us out even further. For example, after a long stretch of studying, our mind is already tired. By scrolling through reels, watching television or texting, we, in a sense, continue to work the same muscle as we were doing before. Coming back from the study break isn't going to make us feel rejuvenated; in fact, we're going to come back even more exhausted than before. It's the same with physical exhaustion as well—going out for a late-night party may not be the best way to recover from a physically taxing day.

The second way in which breaks can have a negative impact is that this inaction can sometimes confront us with difficult emotions that we want to avoid. It can result in us daydreaming, overthinking, or feeling more anxious overall. Again, we don't usually come out of this feeling rejuvenated. We may approach the next task with anxiety, disinterest, or a general sense of fatigue.

How then do we take breaks in ways that can recharge us? The key is active rest. Breaks aren't about inaction, they're about *controlled stillness*. If your mind has been working overtime with academic study, take breaks that involve a more physical activity. Cooking or gardening around the house, playing music or a sport—all of these can get us to start working our body, all the while keeping our mind still (and therefore relaxed) on a single point of focus.

The duration of the break, while important, is still secondary. It's what you do in that break that determines how effective it is. If you want to change your frame of mind, try and switch up the context. An example is when you're taking a break from work, get up from your desk and leave your cabin for a couple of minutes. This quick change in environment is often enough to give our minds a complete break. In situations when it's not possible to physically leave the space, try a moment of visualization—imagine yourself in a calm, relaxed space. Alternatively, use more kinaesthetic mediums like putting down a pen, or stretching or drinking a glass of water, and really focus on the sight, sound, smell, touch and movement, while you're doing these things. If not physically, at least mentally such tasks will remove you from the current mental situation, and allow you to bounce back. Keep in mind, though, that when we talk about visualization, we're not talking about daydreaming, where we zone out uncontrollably while the world is passing us by. We're talking about a brief, controlled strategy where we tune out in a pre-planned manner, at a time that is effective, and bring ourselves back when it matters.

Most of all, when taking a break, avoid things that take you away from your goal. If your aim is to relax, smoking a cigarette is not going to help—in fact, it's going to make you more anxious. If you want to sleep well, alcohol is not going to help—it's going to deteriorate the quality of your sleep. The solution will not be found in shortcuts but in meaningful strategies—and you may take some time to figure out which ones really work for you—that help you recharge and, most importantly, propel you towards your goals.

Podium Finish

1. Active rest is the key to taking breaks.
2. Learn to switch on and switch off to improve focus and prevent fatigue.
3. Plan your breaks: The right kind of break at the right time.

Does the idea of taking
a break stress you out?

18

The Balancing Act: Prioritizing Mental Recovery

'When you get that good sleep...you just feel like, okay, I can tackle this day at the highest level.'

—LeBron James

Simone Manuel, American swimmer and five-time Olympic medallist, is one of those athletes who has been able to come out and speak openly about her health—both physical and mental. In 2021, a few months before the Tokyo Olympic Games, Manuel was diagnosed with Overtraining Syndrome. She was physically exhausted and emotionally depleted, and felt unhappy at the thought of being in the water again. Not taking a break at that moment could have been a career-ending decision.

Why are we talking about overtraining? Because we've all heard that to be the best, we have to give it everything we've got. We've heard of champions being the first ones in for training and the last ones to leave, going that extra mile.

But in this quest for excellence, is there a point where it can become just a bit too much?

It's in a sense similar to burnout. We all have the capacity to recover from short-term stress. In fact, like we've mentioned before, short-term stress can actually be quite helpful to performance. But prolonged stress is a completely different story altogether. Even if not physically straining, what happens to our physical and mental health when we're constantly under pressure, for years on end? Burnout can make us feel emotionally exhausted, cynical and dissatisfied with our lives. And beyond the emotional impact, it can have a very real physical impact too. It can make us prone to aches and pains, illnesses, sleep difficulties, digestive problems, fatigue, and so much more.

Mental Recovery

When we hear the word recovery, we think physical recovery—rest, massages, ice baths, hydration, and so on. The mental side of recovery often goes unrecognized, just as the mental side of performance goes untrained. Or, we simply assume that just because we're lying down and resting, our mind must be relaxing too. Quite the contrary! Being physically inactive and allowing our mind to stew in its thoughts contribute so much more to our stress than we acknowledge. What we don't realize is that cortisol, the hormone associated with stress, counteracts the body's ability to heal. Hence, under stress, the abundance of cortisol flowing through our system results in much slower recovery from fatigue, injuries and illnesses.

A Balanced 'Diet'

Think of life as a plate of food. Even though you may want to become fitter and stronger, you can't just have chunks of protein on your plate. It simply won't work. You're going to need the carbs, fats, fibres, vitamins and minerals too. Similarly, to be successful, you can't fill your life with work alone. To be mentally fit (which is integral to long-term success), you're also going to need a healthy dose of social interactions, hobbies, physical activities and mental stimulation.

Alternate Stressors

You may wonder why these other activities—social interactions, hobbies, and so on—matter when we're talking about success. After all, isn't success about a single-point focus? Aren't all of the rest distractions that disrupt our discipline and get in the way of achieving our long-term goals?

The reason these other activities matter is because all of these other aspects of life also nourish us. They make us stronger and boost our ability to bounce back from setbacks. We already know that outcomes in life aren't in our control, and the trajectory to success is not a linear one. The graph will go up and down, and there will be plenty of time when we need to fall back on our additional resources to cope with these disappointments. It's these other aspects of life that become our buffer, our resources to deal with the hard times.

An Athlete's Identity

Iga Swiatek is one of the few athletes in the world who travel with a full-time sport psychologist. Her psychologist works with her on reaction training, biofeedback and visualization to improve her performance. But there's a lot more that Swiatek does on the mental side to look after herself and her game. In her free time, she's often found playing with Legos, which keeps her engaged and helps her relax. She reads in her downtime and has, on multiple occasions, donated a significant portion of her prize money to not-for-profit organizations that work in the field of mental health. There's so much more to Swiatek than just the person who can run and hit a ball.

'Athlete identity' is a term used to denote the extent to which a player identifies their sense of self with that of an athlete, and how much of their self-worth they derive from their accomplishments in the field. Now, when a player with a strong athlete identity is performing well, their self-confidence is going to be high as well. They're going to feel good about themselves. But what happens when they hit a slump, or experience an injury that forces them out of play?

Over the past few years, researchers have found that players who identify exclusively with being an athlete may be more vulnerable to emotional distress—particularly when they encounter injuries or are dealing with career transitions, like retirement. A person who derives their entire self-worth from their work may feel more imbalanced when encountering difficult situations at work, given that their entire self-worth is seemingly at stake.

When we speak about balance and recovery then, we're talking about seeing ourselves as more than what we do—our sport, our jobs, or any one single aspect of our lives. Of course we give our training our 100 per cent, and of course we play our heart out every time we go out on the field; but to do these things doesn't mean we need to neglect other aspects of our lives. It means prioritizing quality time over quantity, removing time wasters, and investing in the relationships and activities that enrich us.

After all, every relationship, every pursuit of ours, contributes to our sense of self. Each of these allows us to get acquainted with different parts of ourselves. They connect us with strengths we may not have known about and, in that way, add to our overall self-worth. They also make us challenge different parts of our brain and body, keeping us mentally and physically active and balanced.

It's not about a lack of commitment, it's not about preparing to fail. It also doesn't mean that we neglect our priorities. It's about recognizing that a towering building requires a strong foundation, and a strong foundation doesn't come from a single beam alone, no matter how strong. The more pillars we can create for ourselves in our lives, the more resilient that building becomes.

Recovering from a Bad Day

Just like rehabilitation from an ankle injury requires us to strengthen our calf muscles—which aren't the source of the injury directly, but provide strength and support—that's how it also works with emotional distress. Meeting a loved one after a poor result can often soften the blow, help us express ourselves and then bounce back to face another day. Playing with a pet can take away the stressors of a difficult workday.

Exercising can channel the anger we may be experiencing at a situation that hasn't gone our way. Learning a new skill, like mastering a guitar chord, can give us a sense of accomplishment and mastery, which can counter the self-doubt arising from difficulties solving a math problem. Contributing to the community by volunteering, or through simple acts of service, can give us a sense of positivity and make us feel good about ourselves. In fact, another outcome of participating in activities that help others is that it brings about a sense of humility, since it helps take focus away from ourselves and puts our problems in perspective. Events that may have seemed like the end of the world a few moments or hours ago, no longer seem insurmountable.

Creative Distractions

Talking about a sense of balance, a visual that has stayed etched in memory is of Tom Daley, once again by the swimming pool, but this time in the stands at the 2020 Tokyo Olympics. Now the winner of five Olympic medals (including one gold, one silver and three bronze), the British diver was knitting a sweater as he watched a women's synchronized swimming event. In fact, he even shared an Instagram post with the pouch he made for the gold medal he'd won the previous day. He mentioned that knitting had become his way of finding calm, practising mindfulness and relieving stress. It's easy to see how an activity like knitting, rather than becoming a distraction, is actually a strength for an Olympic athlete. Especially during the COVID-19 Olympic Games, which was held in a bio-bubble where athletes weren't allowed to step out or interact with others as much, activities such as these came to the rescue of athletes who wanted to stay engaged, focused and calm.

Sleep for Success

In the kind of hustle culture we've glorified, being sleep-deprived has almost become a kind of flex. People go into work bragging about how little they've slept, and compete for who's the most tired of all. When it's about work, sleep is the first thing to be compromised. When it's for a social life, once more it's the sleep that goes out the window. It's the same to fit in exercise hours. What we lose in hours of sleep, we then try to make up for by downing cups of coffee throughout the day. What ensues is a series of highs and crashes.

You don't have to be an athlete to recognize the importance of sleep. We all need to sleep well to optimize our physical and psychological functioning. Nothing supports recovery quite like sleep. Unfortunately, even if we do want to prioritize sleep, there are now several factors that are a part of our lifestyle that contribute to poor sleep. A sedentary lifestyle, screen habits, caffeine, stress and worry are all aspects that can negatively impact our sleep. If you want to get a good night's sleep, stay off the bed for the rest of the day—no eating, working or lying idle in bed. Sleep is a conditioned response, so being on the bed should be a signal to the brain that it's time to relax and go to sleep. Keep your sleep–awake cycles as consistent as possible, even on weekends. Make sure that you're physically active throughout the day. Keep in mind though that intense exercise in the late hours of the evening can actually worsen sleep, so try exercising earlier in the day if that's a difficulty you struggle with. Avoid too much caffeine, especially during the evening hours—check your supplements for those hidden sources of caffeine we may not always be aware of. Make sure to have a winding-down time about 30–45 minutes before going to bed. Avoid any screens during this time, since they're only going to stimulate your brain further. A warm-water bath, chamomile tea, and soft relaxing music can help set the tone for a more calming environment. Deep breathing and visualizations can help you relax even further. Try reading before going to bed, rather than relying on screens. Reading can take your mind off the worries of the day, slow your thoughts down, and help you drift off to sleep.

Recovery as Training

In our quest for success, it isn't just the hours we put in to train our skill that are important. For this success to be sustainable, you need to start viewing recovery as an integral part of training, not as something you do when it's convenient, or when you're out of options. There is enough evidence across fields that say we perform our best when we pace ourselves, when we take the right breaks, when we replenish ourselves. So yes, to be the best, you have to train the hardest. But what we need is a more comprehensive ethos to training. To be a champion, you also must recover like a champion.

> **Podium Finish**
>
> 1. Mental recovery is just as crucial as physical recovery.
> 2. A balanced and wholesome life is key to long-term success.
> 3. Remember, you are more than what you do.

Think about an experience which shaped you, from which you learnt an invaluable lesson

19

Rolling with the Punches: Overcoming Setbacks

'Success is a process...during that journey sometimes there are stones thrown at you, and you convert them into milestones.'

—Sachin Tendulkar

We all know Sachin Tendulkar as the man who scored a hundred 100s. Recently though, the legend shared the story of how he started his career. Referring to the 'first match of his life', a young Tendulkar invited his friends to watch a match where he was the 'colony's main batsman'. Fortunately or unfortunately, he scored a golden duck that day. Undeterred, he called his friends for the next match to cheer for him once more. The result? Another zero on the first ball. The third time, he didn't call his friends. He stuck it out at the crease for five to six balls and managed to score one run. It may seem like another failure to many, but that young boy went home happy. He'd opened his account, and forever remembered the importance of that one run.

The Inevitable Fall

Highs and lows are a part of life. The highs, we love; the lows, not so much. We like to be good at things, we don't like to fail. A mistake has several emotional associations attached to it. We may feel sad at the loss, or a sense of fear of what may happen next. Feelings of guilt and shame also often accompany the mistakes that we make. And while it's perfectly natural to make mistakes, the problem arises when that mistake—and the emotions associated with it—hijacks our focus from the task. We start replaying the same moment over and over in our minds, hoping and wishing that we'd done something differently. Our mind already starts coming up with excuses that we'll give to others, and to our own selves, about why something didn't work out. Sometimes we may want to give up and leave the field altogether—anything to avoid the intense emotion associated with that mistake. Subsequently, what started as one little mistake snowballs into something much larger.

Stepping Stones

Try to find one athlete, or in fact any person you admire, who has never faced a setback. Someone who has always been perfect and never made a mistake. You're not going to find a single person. Champions aren't people who don't make mistakes. Champions are those who recover faster from mistakes.

The only time you may not make mistakes is if you're doing something that's too easy. Oddly enough though, we do have a tendency to make mistakes even when we're doing something too easy, because it gets boring and we lose our focus. Think about it, would you like to play against an opponent who doesn't stand a chance against you? Again and again? Chances are that you're not going to enjoy it for too long; you might even start dreading it. Why? Because what makes winning exciting is we don't win every time. We enjoy winning because it's *not easy* to win. That's right, easy is boring. It's only when we do something challenging that we're fully engaged and excited. So if you want to succeed, you've first got to befriend failure.

The Mathematics of Mistakes

Think of a game of badminton. It's a race to 21 points. The part we end up ignoring is that we can lose 19 points and still win the game! You don't have to win 100 per cent of the points you play, you only have to reach 51 per cent. And hey, if you get to 54 per cent, you're the GOAT. We're talking here about none other than Roger Federer. If you look at Federer's match statistics, you'll see that he has won 80 per cent of his matches. But look closer and you'll notice that he won only 54 per cent of the points he played! The next time you make a mistake—which yes, you will—keep these numbers in mind.

Build Psychological Flexibility

No matter the amount of effort you put in, there are times you're going to lose in life. It's inevitable. The phrase 'rolling with the punches' comes from boxing jargon. What it means is that when a punch is inevitable, you don't resist it. Instead, you move your body along with the punch. In increasing the time that the punch is in contact with your body, you actually reduce the force of the blow. And it's a good idea to do the same when life throws an unavoidable punch your way.

If you've ever tried to improve your body's flexibility, you would have noticed that your body resists. Every attempt to stretch is pushed back with greater force. The solution is to breathe through the discomfort, let go of the resistance, and let gravity gradually do its job. The mind operates in similar ways, and this is why our ability to adapt to difficult situations has been called 'psychological flexibility'.

How well we deal with mistakes, and adversity in general, depends on how quickly we're able to accept them. And this acceptance is a lot easier said than done. We might ask ourselves, 'How could I do this?' or 'Why did this happen to me?' While these pose as self-reflective questions, they are in fact a form of denial. 'Why me' is resistance, not acceptance— as if answering that question can somehow help change the past. What we need to embrace is the alternative: 'Yes, I did this,' or 'Ok, this has happened.' Suddenly, you're no longer in the past. The resistance is gone. You're now in the present, and your next question is likely to be, 'Ok, so now what can I do next?'

Refrain from Judgement

We don't necessarily fear failure because of failure itself. What we fear a lot more is the judgement that accompanies failure. 'What will people say if they see me making a mistake?' For many of us, it's this fear of shame that drives us to avoid failure at all costs. In fact, this fear often becomes so intense that we avoid playing the game at all. After all, if you don't try, you can't fail. When you evaluate this strategy, you'll realize that failure is inevitable if you don't try. What you think you've avoided is the judgement associated with putting yourself out there and still failing. Versions of this play out in various situations, such as avoiding an exam if you haven't prepared for it, opting out of a presentation because you're underconfident, or even just avoiding conversations in social situations because of the thought 'what if I'm not interesting enough?'

The reason we're talking about judgement is that this judgement doesn't always come from outside. In most cases actually, this judgemental voice is in our own head. In trying to be our most perfect self, our own critical voice is always on alert, waiting to pounce if we make even a single mistake. Next time you make a mistake, notice the voice in your head. Do you hear phrases like 'how could you do this' or 'you're such a failure'? If yes, try and replace that voice with words that are kinder, gentler. At times like this, you don't have to be a strict, reprimanding disciplinarian. What you need is to be your own best friend. If you make a mistake, tell yourself that it's human to make mistakes. Reflect on what you can do better. Remind yourself that it's not over till it's over. Encourage yourself to give the next shot your all.

Learning Moments

If you've seen Tendulkar play a match, then you can't have missed his characteristic shadow batting. Each time he got out, you would see him shadow that shot with the correct technique. Even as he reached the locker room, he'd visualize that ball and shadow what he believed to be the correct shot to play in that instance. From the moment he'd make a mistake, Tendulkar would focus on what he had learnt from that shot, practising to do better next time.

Virender Sehwag too had an interesting take on his so-called failures. Getting out to a bowler didn't faze him. In fact, it gave him the confidence that a ball like that would never get him out again. Now that's the attitude that takes you to two triple centuries.

Stick to the Plan

When preparing for something important, it's likely that you're going to have a game plan. You may have plans A, B and C in case something goes wrong. Often when we make a mistake, we lose confidence in our plan. Rather than sticking to plan A and giving it a real chance, we want to frantically try doing something different. And the real bummer is that we don't just shift to plan B or C; sometimes we just reach a different letter of the alphabet altogether—something that we haven't planned, haven't practised. From doing something we've practised every single day, we start doing something we've pretty much never done before. Just because you've made a mistake doesn't mean that the plan has failed. Persevere. Have faith in your preparation, and stick to your guns. You can always go back to the drawing board later.

Reboot

After making a mistake, we may get stuck in the past, replaying that scene over and over. Or we may start trying too hard. We might try to keep making minor adjustments to our technique with each subsequent event, only making the situation messier.

We've spoken about the concept of switch off–switch on when talking about focus and taking breaks. And here is where it comes into play. To deal with mistakes, treat every moment as an independent one. Don't let any one moment impact the next one. In the words of Roger Federer,

> When you're playing a point, it is the most important thing in the world... But when it's behind you, it's behind you... This mindset is really crucial, because it frees you to fully commit to the next point...and the next one after that with intensity, clarity and focus.

It's okay to allow yourself a moment to feel bad as well. But then, there comes the time to let it go. Feeling 'more bad' doesn't mean that you care more. There's no glory in dwelling in the past; and there are no prizes for feeling bad. So, take a little break between two points. Breathe out the disappointment, breathe in the confidence. Straighten your back and keep your chin up. It's time to take a crack at the next shot.

Podium Finish

1. Mistakes are inevitable. Accept them.
2. Be flexible. Adapt.
3. Learn from the setbacks. Persevere.

Before you begin this chapter, think about what it is that motivates you to pursue your goals. What is it that you want to achieve through these goals?

20

The Inner Drive: Revisiting Motivation

'Racing is the fun part; it's the reward of all the hard work.'

—Kara Goucher

Usain Bolt, in his autobiography *Faster Than Lightning*, wrote,

> I was winning school race after school race. Our house creaked at the fittings with all the plastic trophies and medals I was bringing back...but none of it was really serious to me. I just enjoyed running for fun. I loved the sensation of coming first in school races, of beating the other kids, but there was no way I could have seen that track and field was a serious future for me at that time. How could I? I was just a kid.

I was just a kid...this sentence says it all. Think about the time when you first went out on the playground, or the first time you participated in an event in your school or community, or even the first time you read a book or looked at the night sky through a telescope. Were you thinking about what a champion you would become? Were you daydreaming about the fame and stardom you would experience when you became successful? Or about a fancy car, or a Nobel Prize perhaps?

Nah, we were all just too busy having fun! The joy of being outdoors, running free with our friends, rather than being stuck in classrooms. The joy of hitting a 'boundary' while playing gully cricket. The 'aha moment' when the pieces of a puzzle finally fell into place. The sheer awe and fascination of looking into the vast night sky.

The Why

At some point, as we grew up, things changed. Playing stopped becoming the end goal; it became the means to something else.

Social scientists have labelled these two forms of motivation 'intrinsic' and 'extrinsic'. Intrinsic motivation comes from the nature of the task itself, whereas extrinsic motivation comes from something external to the task, i.e. the rewards associated with carrying out that task.

Extrinsic motivation is easy to recognize, and it's something most of us can relate with. We do things to get good grades, to win medals, to make more money—and these things are important, of course. We work hard so that we can achieve our goals, improve our own quality of life, do the things we want, and look after our loved ones who do so much for us, often sacrificing their own dreams and aspirations so ours can come true. We also want to do well because we receive social rewards—appreciation from friends, family, peers and co-workers. Or perhaps fame and recognition for a job well done. External motivators are powerful tools, there's no doubt about it.

Intrinsic motivation, on the other hand, is a bit harder to identify. Especially in a society which is so achievement-driven, where material things matter so much, what about the task itself that could give us joy? To answer this question, social science researchers have proposed something known as the self-determination theory. According to Richard Ryan and Edward Deci, the answer to finding intrinsic motivation lies in three basic human needs—autonomy, competence and relatedness.

Autonomy: The Need for Control

The world is inherently a chaotic place. There's a lot that goes on that we can't control or predict. It could involve circumstances changing, or people telling us what do to and what not to do. Yet, human beings have a strong desire to be in control, to be responsible for their actions and their outcomes. Thus, autonomy or a sense of agency is a strong human need.

We started this chapter by talking about Usain Bolt and his love for running. And while we all know he's the 'fastest man alive', are you aware that Bolt was born with a condition known as scoliosis, where his spine was bent towards the right side, and his right leg was about half an inch shorter than his left leg? Back pains and frequent hamstring injuries were a result of this condition. To take control of his life, Bolt decided to shrug off the news. He got a coach who understood him and made efforts to understand his physical condition. He realized that he had to strengthen his back and core muscles, and armed with the right kind of knowledge, support systems and dedication, he set off on his journey to becoming the fastest man alive.

If you want to feel intrinsically motivated, take charge. Look out for environments that offer you a sense of autonomy and control. Make decisions, even if they're not always the right ones. This doesn't mean that there will always be a right or a wrong decision; it means that every choice will have its consequences. Let your life be the consequences of your actions.

Competence: The Need to Be Better

Have you ever wondered when you get bored? Yes, the words monotonous or repetitive may come to your mind. But if you really think about it, the times when we're bored are actually times when we're doing something so easy that we don't feel the need to apply ourselves, to put in any significant effort.

I'm sure it sounds counter-intuitive since most of us are looking for ways to make our lives easier. But then, think about the consequence of that—we're also often saddled with a sense of boredom, looking for ways to 'kill time'.

Easy isn't fun, easy isn't challenging. Human beings have a need to gain control and mastery over their environment, to learn new things, and to get better at tasks. It's innate to us. So when you change your orientation to finding joy in learning, in practising so that you're better today than you were yesterday, you're going to get a sense of confidence and satisfaction that's incomparable to others.

When the goal is only to be better than others, you're actually going to select tasks that are easier and require you to put in less effort. Your focus will be on avoiding disappointment rather than on truly getting better. On the other hand, when you set your eyes on improving and learning—being better than your previous self—you're more likely to select challenging tasks, put in more effort, persist despite adversities, and feel more interested in what you're doing. It's also going to be a more controllable and achievable target, which will also reinforce our need for autonomy that we have previously spoken about.

So, don't shy away from trying new things. Don't shy away from things that seem difficult. Even if you feel stuck, stick with it. Persevere. Enjoy the challenge and you will be rewarded.

Relatedness: The Need to Belong

The need to belong is central to human beings. Abraham Maslow has spoken about it in his motivational pyramid: the hierarchy of needs. Being around people and belonging to a social group is rewarding. We're not necessarily talking about structured groups or cliques here. Yes, team sport can have a very positive influence on a person's well-being. But even individual sport allows for a sense of relatedness. It could be the relatedness experienced through a coach or support staff, it could be the feeling of belonging to a particular cohort, or even participating in a competitive activity, where everyone is striving for a common goal. From this relatedness, we derive a sense of respect and self-worth. It gives us an opportunity to care and be cared for, to learn and give back to others as well.

Any task, any activity that we do that provides us an opportunity to relate with others in these ways is rewarding. So it's not just about the task, but also the social environment within which we perform that task. Find activities that offer this avenue of relatedness. Don't think of relationships as distractions from the task. Rather, invest in them, whether at work, at school or back home. The more you look forward to meeting the people you work with, the more you're going to look forward to the work itself.

Changing Motivations

Success can sometimes change us. What starts out as a simple, fun activity can then feel burdened with expectations and fear of disappointments. We no longer play because it's fun, we play to win medals, to get into a good college, or to score an endorsement deal.

We might believe that we're more likely to enjoy a task if we also get rewarded for it. Sounds like a win-win, right? Turns out, this isn't true! In fact, researchers have identified a psychological phenomenon known as the over-justification effect, where our intrinsic motivation to do a task actually reduces after being externally rewarded for it. So if a child loves reading, rewarding them for it can actually diminish the intrinsic value of reading for the child. This explains why so many of us no longer participate in activities and hobbies that once used to give us much joy in and of themselves.

You may argue that we can't stay away from external rewards; we can't deny that they don't matter. We also can't deny that they're going to come our way, whether we like it or not. Even a sports day race in grade one has three players standing on a podium. Competition and comparison are in-built in our society. How do you know then if you're intrinsically or extrinsically motivated? And how do you manage to stay away from the temptations of external rewards?

Ask yourself: Would you still do what you're doing if you weren't receiving a reward for it? If yes, then you're intrinsically motivated. If not, then that's extrinsic motivation right there. At the same time, alter your relationship with that reward that's coming your way. If you see the reward as a source of feedback, of information that you're doing well, then that's going to motivate you intrinsically. If you see the reward as the reason you participate, as the end goal in itself, then that reward will be an extrinsic motivation.

Success vs. Happiness

The last bit of the self-determination theory focuses on relevance. What is the relevance of the goal we have chosen, and where does it come from? Not everybody is motivated in the same way. Different people strive for different things. This idea of personal meaning behind motivation is important, especially in today's world where we're often confronted by the question, 'would you choose success or happiness?' How do we make this trade-off? Frankly though, if we're asking this question, then somewhere perhaps we've gotten lost along the way.

Success is not some standard benchmark that we all have to reach. Success is personal, something that matters to us. If you're working toward something that truly matters to you, and you're succeeding, then you are going to feel happy in any case. On the flip side, it's difficult to feel happy if the things you're doing to be happy take you away from your priorities. Success and happiness go hand in hand. If you're finding a mismatch between the two, perhaps it's time to introspect.

Reconnecting with Purpose

It's possible to be carried away by the web of outcomes. From getting a high from every success and facing a crash after every failure, it's only natural for all of us to experience highs and lows in our lives. At a time like this, take a step back and think about why you're really doing what you're doing. Think about why you set off on this journey in the first place. Allow this sense of purpose to keep you grounded through successes, and fuel your perseverance through disappointments.

Reconnecting with Joy

An interviewer from the *Harvard Business Review* once asked tennis legend Billie Jean King about when she knew she wanted to become a pro tennis player. In response, she narrated a conversation she had in the fifth grade, where she was asked if she wanted to play tennis. 'What's tennis?' she had asked. 'You get to run and hit a ball,' came the explanation. King had then responded, 'Those are my favourite things. I'll try it.'

So, if you find your motivations wavering, think back to why you started doing what you're doing. Think back to the child-like innocence and the joy you experienced. For some time, keep rewards and results on the side, and put away the external consequences. Step away from the stadiums and lights, and return to the gully where you used to play growing up. Take out that old tennis ball and bat, put up those makeshift wickets, call your neighbourhood friends, and reconnect with the joy of playing that six overs one-tip one-hand cricket once again.

> ### Podium Finish
>
> 1. Re-evaluate the importance you give to results.
> 2. Prioritize intrinsic rewards.
> 3. Reconnect with purpose and joy.

In what ways have the expectations of other people impacted your choices and performance?

21

Boos Don't Block Dunks: Handling Social Expectations

'Your love makes me stronger. Your hate makes me unstoppable.'

—Cristiano Ronaldo

The Jumper's Clap

If you've ever watched a track-and-field jumping event—long jump, triple jump, high jump or pole vault—you'll notice an unusual phenomenon. Before starting their run-up for the jump, players often raise their hands up and get the crowds to slow clap with them. As the athletes begin their run-up, the pace of clapping picks up and reaches a crescendo, just as the athletes lift off for the greatest jump of their lives.

We wouldn't be surprised if you haven't watched a jumping event ever before. In fact, given the lack of interest in these events, organizers at one point started drastically cutting down jumping events in track-and-field tournaments. This is part of the origin story of the jumper's clap. Willie Banks, former triple jump record holder, got a rare opportunity to compete in a triple jump event in Stockholm in 1981. Banks went through his standard pre-jump routine of clapping his hands three times and shaking his fists. Something unusual happened this time. Five drunk fans mimicked Banks and clapped three times. Banks got annoyed, found it quite stupid, and went back to focusing on his routine. He clapped three times, and once more the five fans in the stands clapped after him. In that jump, Banks managed to log a distance of 16.88 m. Amazed, he thanked the fans and got started on his next jump. On the second jump, a few more fans joined him. By the third one, in Banks's own words, 'half the stadium was clapping, and in the other half, people were wondering what the hell everyone was clapping for!' As a side note, several track-and-field events take place simultaneously in the stadium, and the jumping events are held on one side of the stadium, so it can be difficult to follow what's going on.

Back to the story, Banks jumped over 17 m and blew kisses to the spectators. Feeling pumped, Banks made an attempt to break some records, and in the fifth jump, landed right next to the world record but unfortunately fouled. Undeterred, despite having fouled, he decided to do a victory lap with one jump still to go! After all, triple jumpers never got to do victory laps like others did. Every part of the stadium he passed, the crowds stood up and clapped for him. For the last jump, everyone started clapping rhythmically, the entire stadium in unison. Banks started running and landed at 17.55 m, just 0.01 m short of his American record.

The story isn't over yet. The year was 1981, and people

in Europe were just starting to watch track-and-field events on television. A week later, Banks competed in the long jump event in Lausanne. Banks was a triple jumper, not a long jumper. He wasn't the greatest long jumper, but the triple jump wasn't an event featured at this tournament (they were cutting back on jumping events, remember). As he raised his hands upwards, everyone in the stadium started clapping rhythmically. Banks didn't see this coming, he couldn't believe it. Yet, that day Banks jumped his personal best and won the competition.

The Social Psychology of Performance

We often think about performance in terms of the individual—their thoughts, efforts and attitudes. And that's what we've been talking about so far in this book as well. But it's time to broaden the scope now, and recognize that performance is not just about one person, but is rather a social construct. Once you give it a thought, it seems quite obvious—the presence and role of other people is what differentiates practice from performance. And so, it's also this presence that likely explains the vast difference in how well a person performs in practice as compared to the actual match days.

Interestingly, the first-ever study in the field of sport psychology is actually one that is also considered to be a seminal work in social psychology. Norman Triplett, an American psychologist, observed that cyclists had better race times when they raced with other cyclists as compared to when they were racing against the clock, trying to beat their personal best. (This probably explains the allure of group spin classes in gyms as well!)

Revisiting the Audience Effect

We have spoken about the 'audience effect' in a previous chapter, but perhaps now is the time to delve into it further. We've all experienced that our behaviour changes when we're being observed by others, compared to when we're by ourselves. But does your performance become better or worse?

The answer lies in how easy or difficult the task is, or rather, how skilled you are at that particular task in question. How does task difficulty interact with being observed? Essentially, what happens is that being in front of an audience increases our arousal levels—the heart rate increases, breathing patterns become a bit shallower, our pitch and volume may change, muscles tighten, and so on. We've all experienced this at several points in our lives. In this state of arousal, we're more alert and more energized. In a state like this, another effect kicks in, known as the 'dominant response effect'. What this means is that under pressure, we are likely to do whatever comes to us more naturally. So, if a task is simple, like running or jumping, we're likely to perform better in front of an audience. On the other hand, if a task is complex, like solving a complex maze, we may tend to make more mistakes.

The differentiating factor then is our skill and our practice. To someone skilled, even complex things may seem easy. So according to the dominant response theory, a novice guitarist may choke under pressure and perform poorly in front of an audience, even when playing something they've learnt before. On the other hand, an expert guitarist may perform even better than they do in practice because of the arousal and energy they receive from the audience.

Home or Away?

There's a lot of debate around the home-ground advantage—do we really perform better when we're in front of our own people or a hostile audience? What the audience effect teaches us is that spectators basically energize us—whether this energy boosts our performance or derails us is then a matter of how we perceive it. If we look at the home crowd as a supportive environment that has our back, we're likely going to give a positive spin to this energy, and use it to improve our performance further. We may also feel the comfort of playing in an environment we're familiar with. On the other hand, if we view the home crowd as people we're afraid to let down, this same advantage can turn into a disadvantage. From playing with excitement, our focus shifts to avoiding disappointment. Every mistake, every silence leads us to want to bury our faces, and run and hide from the shame of letting down our people.

The same is true of the reverse as well. Performing in front of a hostile audience may be a source of threat for sure. It may also become a source of energy, an anger channelled positively, fuelling our desire to perform even better. It may make us work harder to adjust to unfamiliar environments that a home team may take for granted. To understand how to overcome the negative impact of a hostile audience, look no further than Novak Djokovic. Djokovic often felt that the crowds were against him, but each time he felt slighted, he only used that as fuel to assert his dominance on the court!

Practise with an Audience

At the end of the day, it all comes down to perspective, and perhaps a bit of familiarity. Don't throw your hands up in the air because you're going to be in a difficult environment where the odds are stacked against you. Spectators are at worst a distraction, and at best, energizers. Don't focus on the uncontrollable aspect of the crowd. Instead, own it and train with it. The jumper's clap works if you get used to it and train yourself with it. In the absence of that training, it might just throw you off your rhythm.

Practise performing in front of people rather than just by yourself—get used to playing with that level of arousal. If you want to prepare for an interview, ask someone to become that interviewer. If you want to get better at public speaking, initially start speaking in front of a couple of persons. Gradually increase the size of the audience, till the numbers don't faze you anymore. Get comfortable with the reactions people give you and learn to tune them out. Focus instead only on what you are doing, and direct your efforts to getting better.

Stay Away from the Chatter

Being open to feedback is important, but there's a time and place for it. Exposing yourself to unsolicited comments about yourself in the lead-up to a big event is not going to help you. Because, let's face it, even if you get five positive reviews and one negative feedback, your mind is going to focus on the one negative thing you heard or read about yourself, and that's going to impact your entire performance.

It's easy to get swayed by what other people are saying. When India was up against New Zealand in the 2023 Men's World Cup Cricket semi-final, there was so much media speculation about how this would be a repeat of 2019, when India was bowled out, falling short of 18 runs. The discussions centred on how fearful Team India was going to be, going into this match, or how much they had to prove to redeem themselves. Listening to such speculations is hardly ever motivating. They usually have a way of psyching us out, getting us to second-guess ourselves. Speculation is going to develop anticipatory anxiety well ahead of the game, and shift our focus away from our performance to possible results, and the social ramifications of those results.

In this situation and every other that involves such intense media scrutiny, the solution in the locker rooms is simple—stay away from the news channels, stay away from newspapers, and most of all, stay away from social media chatter.

All of these comments that are made, whether on social media or carried through chatter in the hallways, are mere speculations. Nobody can predict the future. This chatter comes from sources that know nothing about you or the efforts you have put in, and they are mere fillers till it's actually time to perform.

There's a difference between feedback and speculation. The speculation needs to be blocked out; the feedback needs to be received at the right time. Right before the big day is usually not that time. Feedback is for after an event, when you're going back to the drawing board, or working on improving your skills over a prolonged period of time—an off-season if you will. Going into a big performance, on the other hand, you need all the confidence you can get. This is not the time to re-evaluate strategy. This is the time to derive confidence from your training, stick to your strategy, double down on your strengths, and get yourself into the zone for success.

Beyond the Expectations Cycle

The better you do, the more people expect. There's never any end to the cycle of expectations. After scoring a century in one match, the pressure to do the same in the next match doesn't come down, it only goes up further. It's sort of like the myth of Sisyphus, who was condemned to roll a boulder up a steep hill, only to have it roll back down and start over again and again.

If people are talking about you, expecting from you, don't let that become a burden you carry. Recognize that it's a part of the journey, and it's often a sign that you're moving up the ladder. It may feel daunting, but remember that the people who talk aren't the same as the people who are out there performing themselves. It's easy to be an armchair critic, viewing things from one's own perspective, without having the entire context. It always helps to know that if you're out there making a presentation, nobody knows the content of that presentation better than you. The audience is looking to *you* for answers. The crowds are watching *you* because they can't do what you do. So, next time you're about to perform in front of an audience, trust yourself, step on to that stage, and let the energy of the crowd power you to your greatest performance.

Podium Finish

1. Performance doesn't depend on an individual alone. Social factors do play a role in it.
2. Learn to train with the pressure; start small.
3. Take expectations and speculations with a pinch of salt.

....

What is your most important
core value? How much
importance do you place on
living your values in your
everyday life?

....

22

The Sporting Spirit: Values for Success

'Courage doesn't mean you don't get afraid. Courage means you don't let fear stop you.'

—Bethany Hamilton

In 2012, during the long-distance run event in Spain, the then Olympic bronze medallist from Kenya Abel Mutai was comfortably in the lead. Trailing behind him in second place was Iván Fernández Anaya from Spain. Just when everyone thought Mutai had this race in his pocket, he slowed down. Unable to understand the signage in Spanish, Mutai mistakenly thought that he'd finished the race. Anaya behind him understood what had happened. Rather than using that opportunity to surpass him and win the gold medal, Anaya chose integrity. He gestured to Mutai and encouraged him to keep running, making sure that Mutai crossed the finish line before him. This gesture may not have won him a gold medal, but that iconic image has certainly found its place in the annals of history.

Several people, including his coach, criticized him for missing out on the opportunity to win. A medal is a medal after all. Anaya's response to the criticism was, 'But what would be the merit of my victory? What would be the honour of that medal? What would my mom think of that? Would my country have felt proud?'

Emotions and Values

Social scientists today distinguish between actions that are guided by our emotions and those guided by our values.

Emotions are a natural, inevitable response to the world around us. When we encounter a threat, we feel scared. When we meet a loved one, we feel happy. Our emotions are automatic, they're not something we need to think through or learn. Yet, our feelings aren't facts: just because we're feeling something, doesn't mean it's true. To understand this better, consider your feelings when you watch a film. A movie can make you laugh, cry or jump with fright. Yet, none of it is really happening; none of it is really real. And still, most of our time these days is spent in running away from, or being overwhelmed by, difficult emotions. We don't want to feel sad, scared or angry, because these are uncomfortable for us.

The other interesting thing about feelings is that they're fleeting—it's possible for us to feel happy, sad and scared all within the span of a minute, depending on whatever the world throws at us.

Values, on the other hand, are more stable. They answer the question of what is most important to us, and they come from within. Our values don't change in response to the world around us.

Self-Worth Revisited

When we choose to respond to our emotions alone, we're all over the place. Because they're so temporary, we're susceptible to the pulls and pushes of the environment. Emotions don't offer stable grounds for action. Subsequently, they don't offer stability in how we think about our own selves. They don't allow us to create a coherent narrative of who we are and what we stand for. And this is why several of the psychological difficulties people experience today have to do with their relationship with their own self.

It's no surprise then that current trends in psychology are moving towards a value-based approach to addressing mental health conditions as well. In fact, from trying to change our thoughts and feelings, the science is now moving towards tolerating these difficult internal experiences, in order to help us lead a life aligned with our values.

It's the same when it comes to performance. It's not possible that we don't experience self-doubt, that we don't experience fear, perhaps even embarrassment. Yet, in that moment, do we choose to respond to the emotion of fear, or do we choose to respond with the value of courage to perform *through* that fear? There may be times in your life when you've picked one or the other. Notice your feelings about yourself when responding to an emotion, and when standing up for your values.

We've spoken about how much our own relationship with ourselves matters when it comes to success. After all, self-confidence is the number one marker for success. Rather than relying on goals and achievements, or fleeting moments of fear and relief—all of which are a lot more fickle in nature—

consider using your values to stay connected with yourself and replenish your self-worth.

Personal Values in Success

Values don't come up that often while talking about success and performance. In fact, our value system hardly ever comes up any time after those grade three moral science classes in school. In fact, ask people what their values are, and most will be stumped. 'I want to come first,' 'I want to be the best,' 'I want to be the youngest director,' etc. We often tend to get confused between our goals and our values. Where goals are a destination, our values are the journey. While we can *achieve* our goals, we *live* our values.

Recognizing Values up Close

Gardner and Moore, authors of *The Psychology of Enhancing Human Performance,* have shared a helpful metaphor to understand values, which is to think of them as a journey. Your destination—or your goal—can be, let's say, to reach Jaipur from Delhi. What would the journey from point A to point B look like though? Will you take a car, a train, or fly there? Let's say you choose to drive. How do you plan to approach that journey? How much and how well do you plan? Do you want to get there as fast as possible? Will you get annoyed at every traffic jam or toll booth you have to stop for? Will you prefer driving at a more comfortable pace, stopping at a *tapri* (shack) to have a cup of tea with some *paratha*s? Will your focus be on overtaking every car that comes your way, or will you make time to appreciate the scenery around you? Will you stop by to help someone in need? What kind of music will you play in the car?

So, you see, life is not just about getting from one place to another. Yes, there are several ways of getting from point A to point B, and all of them will help you achieve that outcome. But *how* you want that journey to be, that's something really worth thinking about, because that's going to determine your entire experience. Our goals are simply the black-and-white outline. It's our value systems that add the colour.

The 'How' of Performance

As an athlete, what do you do if you find out that your competitors are doping? Do you report them? Do you focus on your own game? Do you throw in the towel, thinking there's no point in competing anymore? Do you also participate in doping because this race is really important to you?

Think about a difficult situation you experienced in your own personal or professional life. Reflect on what you thought about it, how you felt, and what decision/s you finally took. What was it that motivated you to make that choice? Looking back, how do you feel about the choice that you made?

It's only natural to experience conflicts in life, or have moments where we want to give up. There's no one clear answer, there are pros and cons to every choice that we make. The problem then is that the fear of consequences often stops us from making decisions, paralyzing us, because these consequences aren't always pleasant.

How do you know if you've made the right choice? You

know when you make a choice that—no matter the material consequences—helps you sleep better at night, that allows you to look yourself in the mirror, stand tall and feel proud of the person you are.

Take a few minutes to sit back and reflect. What are your values? How do you see yourself? Do you think, believe, or see yourself as being honest? Loyal? Hard-working? Disciplined? Resourceful? Helpful? Kind? Authentic? Forgiving? Fun? Generous? Humble? Independent? Open-minded? Patient? Persistent? Responsible? Determined? Agile? The list goes on, but you get the idea.

As you set out to make this list, don't think about what's going to be more socially acceptable, and what your values should be. Be honest with yourself as you reflect on these values. Once you've made your own list—and it doesn't have to be a long one—think about how these values have interacted with the choices you've made in life. You may not be very cognizant about the values you live by, but they've been around for sure, guiding your thoughts and actions.

Beyond Results

Where our goals answer the 'why' of performance, our values inform the 'how'. When someone talks about you, would you like them to say 'oh, they always come first,' or 'their score was xyz'? Or would you want them to talk about how hard-working you are, how fair you are, or how friendly or focused you are? In the chase for results, let's not reduce ourselves to numbers. Let's think beyond results. In fact, let's think beyond goals altogether, and focus on what really, really matters: your character, the person that you are.

People sometimes feel that talking about values is a waste of time, something that slows us down, taking away from the goals we want to reach. On the contrary, our value system is like a compass which guides us to the direction we want to take in life. Rather than reacting to every fleeting emotion, our values keep us steadfast in the direction we want to move in. You may not always have the confidence to succeed, but you still always choose tenacity. These values are our largest reserve of motivation, and so their impact on our performance and long-term success is unequivocal.

Every time you have a difficult choice to make, every time you need to push your limits and step out of your comfort zone, look to your values within to generate that force, that power you need to succeed.

Identify Your Role Models

Do you have a role model? Someone you idolize and want to emulate? Think about what it is that you admire about them, and perhaps note these things down.

Is it their bank balance that you admire? Is it the number of championships they have won? There are a lot of successful people in the world, whether you look at the world of sport, science, business, movies, philanthropy, or any other. What makes us look up to one and not the other is not their achievements alone, but how they reached them. We don't admire report cards and statistics; we admire people and their character.

As you work towards your own path of success, look around you and find a role model you'd want to be like. This doesn't have to be a celebrity, it could be someone you know up close and respect for the way they live their life.

Values for Resilience

We spoke about how our goals are something we achieve, whereas our values are something we live. What this also means is that it's possible to fail when it comes to reaching a goal. And it's possible we may not be able to reach that particular goal ever again. If life is governed by milestones alone, and you haven't reached the milestones you believed you should have, then at some point you feel tempted to give up. But remember that while there may be an expiry date on a certain goal we have, there is never an expiry date on our values. No matter the choices we've made in the past, no matter the outcomes, no matter the mistakes we've made, every moment is a new opportunity to live our values. It's never too late to start. And once you do start, there's no telling how far you may go!

Travel Light

As you move through life, you're going to have a lot of mixed messages coming your way; different people telling you different things, outlining expectations about how you should behave. You've probably been trying to live up to all these expectations in different shapes and forms, all your life! What you will soon realize, if you haven't already, is that you can't live up to everybody's expectations. If your aim is to make everybody happy all the time, it's not going to happen. It's simply not possible. What do we do in such a case? We travel light. After all, who would want to run a marathon with a 30 kg backpack on their shoulders! Strip yourself of these expectations that other people have of you. All you need in this journey are your values. And when you lead a life guided by your values, that's the lightest you're ever going to feel.

Tennis player Jim Courier once said, 'Sportsmanship for me is when a guy walks off the court and you really can't tell whether he won or lost, when he carries himself with pride either way.' How about we adopt this attitude in all aspects of our lives?

Podium Finish

1. Be guided by values, not just goals.
2. It's our values that make us resilient when the going gets tough.
3. Character over results, always.

PART 3

Think about your preparations leading up to an important event. What are the things you did that helped?
What got in the way?

23

A Big Day

In this section, we're going to bring it all together—learnings from the previous two sections—and look at how we can set ourselves up for success on the big day.

Preparing for the Event

Preparation for any event starts with a goal, so set yours at the outset. Also, highlight the values you're going to live by to achieve these goals. Practise: If it's a goal worth achieving, it's going to demand effort, commitment and perseverance from your end. Embrace the monotony, but also keep having fun during practice. Don't just practise the skills; practise how you'll perform the skill with all its uncertainties and pressures. Create scenarios that will challenge you and test you. Most of all, don't forget to train your mind using mindfulness, visualizations, focus, and all the other strategies that we've spoken about.

The journey to success may be long and arduous, and it may be a while till we reach the big day. In the run-up to that day, you may experience moments of confusion and self-doubt. Take feedback, yes, but also self-evaluate. Monitor your own progress, your own efforts. If at the end of the day you are proud of the efforts you've made, then that's all that truly matters.

And remember, pace yourself. The idea isn't to burn out or injure yourself before you get your shot. As you prepare, make time for other meaningful things in your life—your hobbies, your health, and your relationships. All of these are only going to make you physically and mentally stronger. Bring all these together, and you're setting yourself up for that moment of peak performance.

Before the Event

During your preparation, notice the days when you perform the best. What are you doing in the hours before that performance? That's what you need to inculcate into your routine on the day of the event.

You may be tempted to try too hard; perhaps eat something different from what you normally do. People often try to go to sleep earlier than they're used to. This can often be disruptive. Imagine this, you're lying in bed, not sleepy, and all kinds of thoughts and scenarios are barging into your mind. Instead, you need to operate on a sleep cycle that you are comfortable with. Don't go to bed till you're sleepy. Once in bed, some basic visualization and breathing can help you drift off into a restful sleep.

Whether the evening before or the day of the event, make sure to stick to the regular. If you want to strategize about the event, carry out any drills, or visualize, timebox it. Don't let it take over your entire day. Don't allow yourself too much free time to think and ponder.

Engage in basic activities that keep you relaxed yet keep your mind and body busy. A hobby that you enjoy can be helpful. Listening to music, reading and making art can be particularly useful, something that you're not dependent on other people for. If you want to talk to your loved ones, go ahead, but avoid speculating about the event. Don't rely excessively on reassurances from others. It's alright if you're nervous or preoccupied, but use these conversations with people to shift your focus away from the preoccupation.

Do all the things that set you up for a confident day, and don't forget that lucky charm!

Warming up

This is the time to remind yourself of your goals. Not the achievement goals, but the process goals. So, for instance, if you're going in for a public speaking engagement, remind yourself of two to three things that you need to do to speak well. Not things like 'I'll be relaxed,' or 'I'll be confident,' but tangibles like 'I will make eye contact with my audience.' These will keep your focus firmly on controllable processes, and away from self-doubting thoughts.

An affirmation at this time will also help. Say something positive to yourself, something that makes you feel strong, powerful or calm—whatever it is that you want to feel that day. And that brings us to the last part of the warm-up. Get yourself in the right energy zone. We've spoken about psyching up and psyching down; this is where you have to use those strategies. Whether it's breathing, music, social interactions, visualizations or physical movements, use the techniques that work for you to get yourself into that optimal zone of functioning.

During the Event

As you begin the event, follow your pre-performance routine. This is going to help you zone in and focus on what you need to be focusing on, the controllables. Don't give yourself too many instructions at this point. Remember, just a cue word, followed by a powerful exhalation, and off you go!

Through hits and misses, stick to your game plan. Keep your body language positive, and maintain your rhythm. If one thing hasn't gone your way, don't brood over it. Switch off, switch on, and take another crack at it.

Remember what we've been talking about: it's normal to feel the pressure. However, you have an entire arsenal—you've trained all the skills and techniques that it takes to cope with the pressure that's coming your way. So don't shy away from it. Soak up the pressure, embrace it, and most of all, enjoy it!

After the Event

When we speak of performance, we don't often talk about the phase after the event. In fact, several elite athletes have referred to this as the 'post-Olympic blues'. What's important to remember here is that these players don't experience these blues when they lose, they can also experience them after a win.

Addressing the aftermath of the event is important because it determines our approach to wins and losses, and subsequently our future performance. After all, no single event is the be-all and end-all of life. You're still going to get up the next day and move forward with your life.

It's only natural to feel jubilant after a win and sombre after a loss. Allow yourself to feel these feelings, but don't allow them to go on forever. It can be for a few minutes or a few hours, but remember, the faster you're able to move on from your emotions, the more psychologically agile you're going to be.

Regardless of your performance, make some plans for how you'd like to spend the rest of the day, or perhaps even the next few days. You've put in the work, so you deserve the break, no matter the performance.

When you talk about the event, don't just talk about the result. There's no story when all you say is 'I won'. Talk about your experience; share the highs and lows. In fact, as you reflect on the experience, think about three things—what you did well, what you learnt, and what you need to work on next time. Just because you lost doesn't mean you did nothing well. And just because you won doesn't mean that you have nothing to learn and nowhere to grow from the experience.

Don't withdraw, don't isolate. Face the world, and be proud of your efforts. And once your post-event analysis is done, set your sights on the next target and return to your routine. Even if you become a world champion, tomorrow is a fresh start—a clean slate, a new day!

What is your mantra for success?

24

The Winning Attitude

It's what we started with, and it's what we're going to end with. Champions are brilliant at the basics. You have all of these skills at your disposal, and what you need to bring it all together is that winning attitude.

What is that winning attitude all about? Determining your own destiny, making your own goals, and living by values that are true to you. Commit to your goals and then persevere. Prepare well and practise hard.

Don't let a single moment define you. Don't get carried away by short-term temptations and distractions; set yourself up for long-term success. Give it your all, but as you learn to win, also learn to lose. Take both wins and losses in your stride. We all get knocked down, but what's important is getting back up. Perfection is overrated; be open to learning, be curious, and be willing to accept what you don't know.

And while no single moment defines us, every moment matters. Whether it's a love-all or a match point, approach both with the same focus and intensity. Respect every adversary and the efforts they've put in. Learn from everyone, but don't let that respect undermine your own worth.

Adapt to whatever situations life throws at you. Be an optimist and believe. Look for the positives amidst all the negativity that also surrounds us. Play the game with the right spirit, so you can look back at it with your head held high. Don't let scoreboards and statistics determine your self-worth. Remember, you got this. You are enough.